Nita Mehta's
Perfect Vegetarian cookery

Nita Mehta

M.Sc. (Food & Nutrition), Gold Medalist

SNAB
Publishers Pvt. Ltd.

LAKSHMI BOOK STORE
18, Janpath Bhawan
Janpath, New Delhi-110001
☎ 23718152, 23327181

Nita Mehta's
Perfect Vegetarian
cookery

© Copyright 1999-2002 **SNAB** Publishers Pvt Ltd

WORLD RIGHTS RESERVED: The contents - all recipes, photographs and drawings are original and copyrighted. No portion of this book shall be reproduced, stored in a retrieval system or transmitted by any means, electronic, mechanical, photocopying, recording or otherwise, without the written permission of the publishers.

While every precaution is taken in the preparation of this book, the publishers and the author assume no responsibility for errors or omissions. Neither is any liability assumed for damages resulting from the use of information contained herein.

TRADEMARKS ACKNOWLEDGED: Trademarks used, if any, are acknowledged as trademarks of their respective owners. These are used as reference only and no trademark infringement is intended upon.

3rd Reprint 2002

ISBN 81-86004-92-0

Food Styling & Photography: **SNAB**

Layout and laser typesetting:

National Information
Technology Academy
3A/3, Asaf Ali Road
New Delhi-110002
☎ 3252948

Published by:

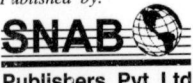

Publishers Pvt Ltd
3A/3 Asaf Ali Road
New Delhi-110002

Editorial and Marketing office:
E-348, Greater Kailash-II, N.Delhi-48
Fax: 91-11-6235218 Tel: 91-11-6214011, 6238727
E-Mail: nitamehta@email.com
snab@snabindia.com

The Best of Cookery Books *Website*: http://www.nitamehta.com
Website: http://www.snabindia.com

Printed at:
THOMSON PRESS (INDIA) LIMITED

Distributed by:
THE VARIETY BOOK DEPOT
A.V.G. Bhavan, M 3 Con Circus
New Delhi - 110 001
Tel: 3327175, 3322567; Fax: 3714335

Price: Rs.189/-

With love to my dear sister-in-law

Anu Kshetrapal

who has been of immense help in the writing of this book.

Tips To Throw A Successful Party

Are you planning to throw a dinner party? Let this not worry you any more.

For serving good food, a well prepared menu is important. Plan your menu well so that you are CLEAR in your MIND, what to cook. This will help you to do your shopping properly, without having to run to the market at the last minute. While planning the menu, keep in mind that the dishes differ in taste and colour. A dish may be sour with the taste of tomatoes or yogurt, another spicy with masalas and yet another with a hint of sweetness of coconut or honey. Prepare your food imaginatively and garnish them differently. Do not try out a new recipe on the day of the party because you are not sure of it's taste and looks. Try new recipes when you have ample time and no tension.

Serve food in a pleasant atmosphere. Cheer up your rooms by keeping a few flowers, which can be bought from a florist a day before the party. Spread a smart dinning sheet with matching, well starched napkins. It's the total atmosphere that counts - just dumping good food on the table is not enough!

Be organized in your affairs. Count the number of guests and see that you have that many plates and spoons on the table. Stack your dessert plates and spoons before the dinner.

Last but not the least, always be ready and well dressed on time to give your guests a warm welcome with a smile. You may wear the most exotic jewellery and clothes, serve the most delicious food, but if the SMILE is missing and you are not pleasant to talk to, nobody really enjoys the party. Give the same warm welcome to both old & young.

Nita Mehta

Exciting Raitas 91

    Mixed Vegetable Raita   92
    Mint Raita   93
    Raita Anaarkali   93
    Attractive Papadi Raita   94
    Dahi-Bhalle Bemisaal   96
    Baghara Raita   98
    Peanut Raita   98

Chaawal - Roti 99

    Paneer & Mushroom Pulao   100
    Mixed Vegetable Pulao   101
    Lemon Rice   102
    Missi Roti   103
    Vegetable Biryani   104
    Methi Wali Puri Aur Parantha   105
    Vegetable Fried Rice   106

Desserts - Puddings 107

    Apple Stew with Rabri   108
    Date & Walnut Pudding   111
    Ice Cream with Apples in hot cherry sauce   112
    Strawberry Ripple Pudding   113
    Mango Pie   114
    Chocolate Exotica   116
    Baked Guavas with Cream   118
    Orange Turn About   119
    Pineapple Trifle   120
    Shahi Kulfi   121
    Shahi Kulfi-II   122
    Chocolate Pudding   123
    Cake n' Ice Cream Fantasia   124
    Malpuas   125
    Special Rice-Kheer   126
    Crumbly Grape Pudding   127

Names Of Ingredients

INDIAN NAME	ENGLISH NAME
Ajwain	Carom seeds
Aloo	Potato
Amchoor	Dried mango powder
Anaar	Pomegranate
Anaardana	Pomegranate seeds
Arbi	Colocasia
Arhar ki dal	Yellow lentil
Atta	Whole wheat flour
Badaam	Almonds
Baingan	Brinjal
Besan	Gram flour
Bhindi	Lady's finger
Channa	Bengal gram
Channe ki dal	Split gram
Chillah	Pancake
Dahi	Yogurt
Dalchini	Cinnamon
Dhania	Coriander
Dhania saboot	Coriander seeds
Garam masala	Mixed spices
Gobhi	Cauliflower
Haldi	Turmeric
Hing	Asafoetida
Chhoti illaichi	Green cardamom
Imli	Tamarind
Kaju	Cashew nut
Kala-namak	Rock salt
Kale channe	Black gram
Kali mirch	Black pepper
Kali mirch saboot	Peppercorns
Kalonji	Nigella seeds, Onion seeds

INDIAN NAME	ENGLISH NAME
Karela	Bitter gourd
Kasoori methi	Dry fenugreek leaves
Kesar	Saffron
Kheera	Cucumber
Khoya	Dried whole milk
Khus-khus	Poppy seeds
Kishmish	Raisins
Laung	Cloves
Magaz	Kernels of seeds of cucumber, melon, water melon and pumpkin mixed together
Maida	Plain flour
Malai	Milk topping
Matar	Peas
Methi dana	Fenugreek seeds
Mooli	Radish
Moong ki dal	Split green gram
Moti illaichi	Brown cardamom
Nariyal	Coconut
Paalak	Spinach
Paneer	Cottage cheese
Pista	Pistachio
Poodina	Mint leaves
Rajmah	Kidney beans
Raita	Yogurt flavoured with spices
Saunf	Fennel seeds
Seviyan	Vermicelli
Sirka	Vinegar
Suji	Semolina
Tej patta	Bay leaf
Til	Sesame seeds
Urad dhuli	Split black beans
Urad saboot	whole black beans
Zeera	Cumin seeds

Party Tips

Substitutes

Sometimes it happens that one suddenly realizes that one ingredient is missing. The following are substitutes which may come handy.

Item	Substitutes
1 tbsp cornflour	2 tbsp maida (as a thickening agent)
1 tsp baking powder	2 tsp soda-bicarb (mitha soda)
1 cup fresh milk	4 tbsp powdered whole milk + 1 cup water
1 cup cream	3/4 cup skimmed milk and 1/3 cup butter
30 gm chocolate (solid)	3 tbsp cocoa + 1 tsp fat
2 tsp arrowroot	2 tbsp flour (as a thickening agent, also gives a gloss)
1 cup self raising flour	1 cup flour + 2 tsp baking powder
2 tsp drinking chocolate	1 tsp cocoa + 1 tsp sugar

Approximate quantities for a party

Item	Serving	Quantity
Tea	25 cups	40 gms tea leaves
Coffee	25 cups	75 gms instant coffee
Squash	20 glasses	1 bottle
Bread	24 slices	1 large
Sandwiches	24 pieces	1 large bread
Butter	24 slices	100 gms
Rice (Basmati)	4 servings	1 cup
Rice (Basmati)	25 people	1 ½ kg
Dry vegetable preparation	25 people	2 kg
Dals	25 people	750 gms
Potato chips	25 people	1 kg
Ice cream	25 people	4 litres
Cake	25 people	1½ kg

A safe way to calculate for big parties, where the variety is fairly large, is to work out helpings at 1½ times the number of people, for e.g. 40 people / 60 sandwiches.

Culinary Terms

Bake	To cook by dry heat usually in an oven or tandoor.
Batter	Any mixture of flour and a liquid such that it can be beaten or stirred and can be poured.
Beat	To mix with a fast rotatory motion so that air is incorporated into the mixture. Beating makes the mixture light and fluffy.
Blanch	To remove skin by dipping into hot water. e.g. to blanch tomatoes or almonds.
Blend	To combine two or more ingredients.
Consistency	A term describing the texture, usually the thickness of a mixture.
Cut and fold	To mix flour very gently into a mixture using a downward and upward movement.
To Dust	To sprinkle flour in an empty greased tin so that the cake does not stick to the tin after it is baked.
Dot	To put small amounts of butter.
Dice	To cut into small neat cubes.
Dough	A mixture of flour, liquid etc., kneaded together into a stiff paste or roll.
Drain	To remove liquid from food.
Garnish	To decorate.
Marinate	To soak food in a mixture for some time so that the flavour of the mixture penetrates into the food.
Puree	A smooth mixture obtained by rubbing cooked vegetables or blanched tomatoes through a sieve.
Saute	To toss and make light brown in shallow fat.
Shred	To cut into thin long strips.
Sift	To pass dry ingredients through a fine sieve.
Toss	To lightly mix ingredients without mashing them e.g. for salads.
Whip	To incorporate air by beating and thus increase the volume as in egg whites and whipped cream.

Weights and Measures

Use a tea cup for measuring

A table spoon is written as tbsp, a teaspoon as tsp.

Food stuff	Measure	Weight (gms)
Cereals		
Rice	1 cup	125
Atta (wheat flour)	1 cup	100
Maida (plain flour)	1 cup	100
Suji	1 cup	120
Dals (Pulses)		
Average for all dals	1/3 cup	50
Rajmah	1 cup	125
Channa	1 cup	125
Besan	3/4 cup	50
Dairy Products		
Milk	1 cup	200
Milk Powder	1/4 cup	20
Cheese grated	1 tbsp	5
Butter	1 cup	150
	1 tbsp	15
Curd	1/2 cup	100
	1 tbsp	15
Cream	1/2 cup	100
	1 tbsp	15
Fats and Oils		
Refined oil	1 cup	150
	1 tbsp	15
Ghee	1 cup	180
	1 tbsp	15

Food stuff	Measure	Weight (gms)
Nuts		
Ground nuts	1 tbsp (37 pieces)	10
	1/4 cup	40
Almonds	9 big	10
Cashewnut	6 large	10
Walnut	4 halves	10
Raisins	1 tbsp	10
Pista	1 tbsp (18 pieces)	10
Desiccated coconut	1/2 cup	25
Miscellaneous		
Tea leaves	1 tsp	1.5
Cocoa powder	1 tbsp	5
Coffee powder	1 tbsp	2
Custard powder	1 tbsp	6
Cornflour	1 tbsp	6
Creamed Corn	1 tbsp	17
Gelatine	1 tbsp	5
Sugar	3/4 cup	100
Icing Sugar	1/4 cup	30
Vegetables		
Kheera (cucumber)	1 medium	150
Peas	10 Pods	50 (edible-25)
French beans	13	50
Ginger	1" piece	10
Tomato	1 medium	50
Potato	1 medium	70
Onion	1 medium	60
Cauliflower	1 medium	400
Mushroom	7 medium	100
Cabbage	1 medium	400
Carrot	1 medium	60

Scrumptious Breakfast

Here are a few recipes for the main breakfast items. Fruits, sweetmeats, tea and coffee are of course served as accompaniments.

A filling breakfast is essential, but it should be simple enough to be prepared quickly in the morning. A few sweetmeats have been included, incase it is difficult to go to the Mithai-wala during the busy morning hours.

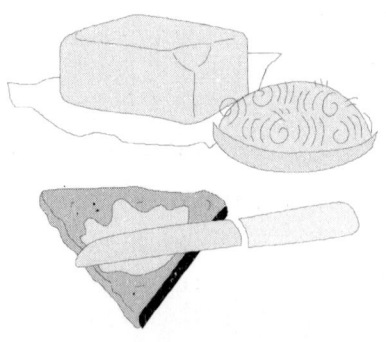

Paalak-Paneer Toasts

Servings 4

- A perfect fusion of Indian Paneer and western Mozzarella cheese on toast. The spinach adds to the taste and colour.

INGREDIENTS

1½ tbsp butter
4 slices brown bread
½ tsp crushed garlic
100 gm (25-30) leaves of paalak (spinach) - washed & shredded
150 gm paneer (cottage cheese)
5 tbsp mozzarella cheese (Amul) - grated
1 tbsp chopped coriander
¼ tsp salt and pepper, or to taste
¼ tsp red chilli flakes

METHOD

1. Wash and shred spinach leaves into thin ribbons.
2. Heat butter in a kadhai or pan. Add crushed garlic and stir. Add spinach and cook till all the moisture of the spinach evaporates. Remove from heat.
4. Mix grated paneer, coriander and 4 tbsp grated mozzarella cheese, leaving behind 1 tbsp for the topping.
5. Add cooked spinach to the paneer and mix well. Add salt and pepper.
6. Toast the slices and spread the mixture on the toasts. Sprinkle some mozzarella cheese. Sprinkle some red chilli flakes too.
7. Grill in an oven at (210°C) for 2-3 minutes. Cut into triangles and serve hot.

Toast Bonanza

Picture on facing page

Servings 8 toasts

- Bread topped with various fillings and covered with cheese.

INGREDIENTS

200 gms Pizza cheese or mozzarella cheese
1 small cabbage
3-4 firm tomatoes - cut into slices
2 big boiled potatoes
250 gms *paneer* (cottage cheese)
salt, pepper to taste
3-4 tbsp butter
8 bread slices

METHOD

1. Cut *paneer* and potatoes into thin slices.
2. Heat 2 tbsp butter in a nonstick pan. Put a slice of potato on it and then shift to the side. Turn when the under side is light brown.
3. Repeat with the other potato slices. Let them be on the sides of the pan.
4. Put some more butter. Saute the *paneer* slightly. Remove from heat.
5. Lightly toast the bread slices. Remove crust. Butter them.
6. On each toast spread a cabbage leaf.
7. Cover the leaf with 2 potato slices. Sprinkle salt and pepper.
8. Put *paneer* slices over the potatoes.
9. Put tomato slices over the *paneer*.
10. Grate cheese to cover the tomatoes almost completely.
11. Grill in a preheated oven for about 5 minutes till the cheese melts and gets browned a little.
12. Serve immediately surrounded by a few cabbage leaves made crisp by dipping in chilled water for half an hour.

Note : Use only pizza or mozzarella cheese, i.e. the type of cheese should be such that it melts on heating.

1. Chillah Vilayati	- Recipe on page 21
2. Toast Bonanza	- Recipe on page 18

Rajasthani Chillah

Picture on cover

Servings 10-12 chillahs

- Moong dal imparts a special flavour to the chillahs.

INGREDIENTS

for the chillah

1 cup *dhuli moong dal* (split green beans)
2 tbsp fresh coriander - chopped very finely
2 green chillies - deseeded & chopped very finely
1 tsp salt
½ tsp red chilli powder

for the filling

150-200 gms *paneer* (cottage cheese) - cut into 3" long fingers
2 tbsp oil
½ tsp salt
½ tsp *garam masala* (mixed spices)
½ tsp red chilli powder
1 tbsp chopped coriander

METHOD

1. Soak *dal* for 3-4 hours only, (not overnight).
2. Strain. Grind with 1 cup water to a smooth batter. Add about ½ cup water to get a pouring consistency. Add salt, chilli powder, coriander and green chillies. Keep aside.
3. Prepare the *paneer* by heating 2 tbsp oil in a non-stick pan. Add ½ tsp salt, *garam masala* and red chilli powder. Put off the gas. Add *paneer* pieces and coriander. Mix gently with the oil. Return to fire, saute for a few seconds. Keep aside.
4. Heat a non-stick pan (not too hot), smear 1 tsp oil in the centre. Spread one *karchi* (¼ cup) of batter to make a *chillah* of about 4" diameter. Pour some oil on the sides. Turn over.
5. Heat one prepared *paneer* piece on the side of the pan. Place the *paneer* piece at one end of the *chillah*. Roll it up. Serve hot with poodina chutney or any other sauce.
6. To make the next chillah, turn off the gas. Cool the pan by sprinkling some water. Wipe clean. Smear 1 tsp oil in the centre. Spread 1 *karchi* of batter. Return to fire & proceed as above.

Note: To prepare chillahs for breakfast, it is better to soak the dal in the evening, grind it at night and keep in the fridge. Use it to make chillahs the next morning.

C̲ʜɪʟʟᴀʜ V̲ɪʟᴀʏᴀᴛɪ

Servings 2 *Picture on page 19*

- The Indian pancake turned Western!

INGREDIENTS

for the batter

3/4 cup *besan* (gram flour)
1 cup water (approx)
¼ tsp red chilli powder
½ tsp salt

for the filling

1 onion - finely chopped
1 tomato - finely chopped
1 green chilli - finely chopped
1 tbsp chopped coriander
salt and pepper to taste

METHOD

1. Mix all ingredients of the batter together to make a batter of pouring consistency.
2. Mix all ingredients of the filling. Add salt & pepper to taste.
3. Heat a non-stick pan (not too hot). Smear 1 tsp oil in the centre.
4. Remove from fire and spread 1½ *karchis* (1/3 cup) of batter. Spread by tilting the pan.
5. Return to fire. Add 1 tbsp of oil on the sides and on the surface of the chillah.
6. Turn over when the underside is done. Cook the other side.
7. Turn again. Put half of the filling in the centre.
8. Fold the right and the left sides like a dosa.
9. Serve immediately with tomato ketchup or mint chutney.

Layered Pancakes

Servings 6-8

- Ideal when there are a number of people sitting down for breakfast together

INGREDIENTS

for the pancakes

1½ cups *maida* (plain flour)
2¼ - 2½ cups milk
1 tsp salt
½ tsp pepper
¼ tsp *mitha soda* (soda bicarb)

for the filling

200 gm *paneer* (cottage cheese) - cut into flat, thin and small pieces
1 big boiled potato - mashed coarsely
3 onions - chopped finely
2 green chillies - chopped
¼ tsp *haldi* (turmeric pd.)
½ tsp red chilli powder
salt, pepper to taste
3 tbsp oil

METHOD

for the pancakes

1. Sift *maida* and salt.
2. Mix all the other ingredients. Beat well with an egg-beater. Add enough milk to get a pouring consistency.
3. Heat a non-stick pan (not too hot). Smear ½ tsp oil on it in the centre.
4. Remove from fire and pour 1/3 cup (1 big *karchi*) batter. Tilt the pan to spread the batter. Return to fire.
5. Turn the pancake when the under side is cooked. When the other side is cooked, remove from pan and keep aside.
6. Make 6-7 such pancakes.

for the filling

1. Cook onions in oil till transparent.
2. Add *haldi* and red chillies.
3. Add the potatoes. Cook on slow fire for ½ minute.
4. Add *paneer* and green chillies.
5. Add salt, pepper to taste.
6. Remove from fire.

Contd...

METHOD

to assemble the pancakes

1. Place a pancake on a greased stainless steel plate.
2. Spread some filling over it.
3. Cover with another pancake. Press well.
4. Repeat in the same way, ending with a pancake. Press well.
5. Cut the stacked pancakes with any round stainless steel box with a sharp edge of about 7-8" diameter, to give the pancakes a neat look.
6. To serve, heat in an oven for 7-8 minutes by covering the pancakes with aluminium foil or microwave for 3 minutes without covering.
7. Some processed cheese may be grated on the pancakes before heating them in the oven.

Note:
- **The pancakes tend to get dry & extra crisp if heated in the oven without covering them.**
- **Serve with a sharp edged flat serving spoon so that it can be cut as well as served with it.**

Utthapam Special

Picture on facing page

Servings 15

- The simplest South Indian breakfast.

INGREDIENTS

for the batter

3 cups uncooked rice
1 cup *dhuli urad dal* (split black beans)
1 tsp *methi dana* (fenugreek seeds)
3 tsp salt

for the topping

3 onions - chopped finely
3 tomatoes - chopped finely
2 carrots - grated
½ small cabbage - chopped finely
2 green chillies - chopped finely
salt to taste

METHOD

for the batter

1. Soak *dal* with *methi dana* and rice separately for 10-12 hours or overnight.
2. Grind rice and *dal* separately.
3. Mix the two together. Add salt.
4. Keep the batter in a warm place for 8-10 hours to ferment. If the batter does not rise, add ½ tsp soda bicarb, at the time of making the utthapam.
5. The batter should be of a pouring consistency, but not very thin, so add water accordingly, at the time of making the utthapam.

to prepare the utthapam

1. Mix all ingredients of the topping.
2. Heat a non-stick pan. Smear ½ tsp oil on it.
3. Remove from fire. Spread 2 *karchis* (½ cup) of batter.
4. Return to fire. After a few seconds, sprinkle vegetables. Press a little.
5. Pour a little oil on the utthapam and the sides.

Contd...

1. Lemon Rice — Recipe on page 102
2. Utthapam Special — Recipe on page 24
3. Coconut Chutney — Recipe on page 26
4. Sambhar — Recipe on page 31

METHOD

6. Turn when the underside is cooked. Cook for 1-2 minutes.
7. Remove from pan and serve hot with coconut chutney as given below, made with fresh coconut or dry coconut powder.

Coconut Chutney

Picture on page 25

INGREDIENTS

½ cup desiccated or fresh coconut
¼ cup roasted *bhune channe* (bengal gram) or *channa dal* (split gram)
1 green chilli - chopped
1 onion - chopped
3/4 tsp salt
¼" piece ginger
2 flakes garlic (optional)
1 cup sour curd (approx.)

for baghar

1 tbsp oil
1 tsp *rai* (mustard seeds)
1-2 dried, whole red chillies

METHOD

1. Mix all ingredients.
2. Grind, adding enough curd to get a soft dropping consistency.
3. Put in a bowl and keep aside.
4. In a separate pan, heat 1 tbsp oil. Add 1 tsp mustard seeds.
5. When they splutter, add 1 to 2 broken dried red chillies.
6. Add this oil to the chutney. Mix well.

Vegetable Cutlets with Glazed Vegetables

Servings 4 pieces

- A sumptuous breakfast when served with buttered toasts.

INGREDIENTS

for the cutlets

2 big potatoes
2 small carrots
10-12 french beans or ½ cup peas
2 green chillies - chopped
½ tsp salt
½ tsp *garam masala* (mixed spices)
½ tsp black pepper
½ tsp *zeera* (cumin seeds)
4 tbsp dry bread crumbs
4 tsp *maida* (plain flour)
oil for shallow frying
4 tbsp crushed cornflakes

METHOD

for the cutlets

1. Boil potatoes and mash them.
2. String french beans, scrape carrots.
3. Chop french beans and carrots finely.
4. Pressure cook beans and carrots with 1/3 cup water.
5. After the first whistle pressure cook for 2-3 minutes, on low heat.
6. Remove from fire. When cool, mash the vegetables. (If there is water, mash the vegetables on fire so that the water dries up while the vegetables are being mashed).
7. Mix mashed potatoes, green chillies, bread crumbs, *zeera*, *garam masala* & black pepper with the mashed vegetables.
8. Form into heart shaped cutlets.
9. Make a paste of 4 tsp *maida* with 4 tbsp water.
10. Coat the cutlets with *maida* paste, roll in crushed cornflakes or bread crumbs.
11. Shallow fry in a pan till crisp and golden.
12. Serve with boiled and glazed vegetables as given on the next page.

Contd...

Boiled & Glazed Vegetables

Servings 2

- Serve with vegetable cutlets.

INGREDIENTS

½ of a small cauliflower
1 carrot
6-8 french beans
1 tbsp salted butter
½ tsp sugar
1 tsp salt
a pinch of salt & pepper

METHOD

1. Cut cauliflower into big florets and carrot into thin long pieces. String beans, cut diagonally into 1" pieces.
2. Boil 3-4 cups water with 1 tsp salt and ½ tsp sugar.
3. Add cauliflower, carrot and beans.
4. Boil till just tender. Do not over boil.
5. Heat 1 tbsp of butter with ½ tsp of sugar and toss the boiled vegetables in it. Add salt, pepper to taste.
6. To serve bread with the cutlets, butter a toasted slice and cut into 2 triangular pieces like a sandwich.
7. Serve cutlets with these vegetables and toasts to make it a complete breakfast.

Stuffed Bread

Servings 4

- A perfect harmony of Indian and Western food!

INGREDIENTS

1 unsliced bakery bread (small)
salted butter 25 gms (2tbsp)

for the filling

3 potatoes - boiled and mashed coarsely
1 cup shelled peas
2 onions - chopped very finely
2 tomatoes - chopped finely
2 green chillies - chopped very finely
5 tbsp oil
¼ tsp *haldi* (turmeric powder)
½ tsp red chilli powder
1 tsp salt (to taste)
½ tsp *garam masala*

METHOD

1. Make a hole of 1½" x 2" on each side of the bread.
2. Scoop out the bread leaving about ½" of the bread, on all four sides. Keep aside.
3. Heat oil. Add onions. Cook till light brown.
4. Add *haldi* and red chilli powder. Cook for a few seconds.
5. Add tomatoes & cook on slow fire till oil separates. Mash them well.
6. Add the peas. Add salt, green chillies & *garam masala*. Cook till peas are done.
7. Mash half of the scooped out bread, and add to the peas. Cook for a few minutes on low heat.
8. Add the potatoes. Mix well for a few minutes.
9. Add more salt if required. Remove from fire.
10. Butter the outside surface of the scooped out bread loaf on all four sides. Close one end with the cut piece of bread.
11. Put in the filling nicely. Keep pressing while putting in the filling. Turn the bread and fill from the other side also after pressing.
12. Close the other hole too.
13. Heat in a hot oven for 15 minutes before serving.
14. At the time of serving, cut out slices of 3/4" thickness with a sharp knife.
15. Serve with tomato ketchup.

Vada with Sambhar and Coconut Chutney

Servings 15-20

- The ideal breakfast for a large crowd.

INGREDIENTS

2 cups *urad dhuli dal* (split black beans)
3 green chillies - chopped
½" piece ginger - chopped
2 big onions - chopped finely
salt to taste
2 tbsp besan (gram flour)
oil for deep frying

METHOD

1. Clean, wash and soak *dal* for 2-3 hours only. Do **not** over soak.
2. Strain the *dal*, add ginger and green chillies. Grind to a paste using the minimum amount of water in the mixer.
3. Add the onions, besan and salt to taste.
4. Beat the mixture with an electric egg beater for 2-3 minutes or with the hand for at least 4-5 minutes. (This step is important).
5. Heat oil to medium hot.
6. Wet your palm of the left hand, place a ball of the *dal*, wet the first finger of the right hand and make a hole in the *vada*.
7. Wet your right hand fingers, gently transfer the *vada* on the right hand fingers.
8. Carefully slip the *vada* into the hot oil with the help of the thumb.
9. Fry 6-7 *vadas* together, till golden brown.
10. Serve with sambhar as given on the next page and coconut chutney, given on page 26.

Contd...

Sambhar

Picture on page 25

INGREDIENTS

1 cup *arhar ki dal* (yellow lentil)
a small lemon sized ball of *imli* (tamarind)
5-6 flakes garlic - chopped
½" piece ginger - chopped
2 tbsp sambar powder
2 onions - cut into thin slices
½ tsp *rai* (mustard seeds)
½ tsp *zeera* (cumin seeds)
2 whole dried red chillies
salt to taste

METHOD

1. Clean, wash and pressure cook *dal* with 4 cups water and 1 tsp salt.
2. After the first whistle, keep on slow fire for 20 minutes.
3. Wash *imli*. Boil with 1 cup water. Cool. Extract the pulp. Keep aside.
4. Crush garlic and ginger roughly to a paste.
5. Heat 4 tbsp oil. Add *rai, zeera* and dried red chillies broken into bits.
6. Add the onions. Cook on low heat till onions turn dark brown. (Do not burn them).
7. Add *imli* extract. Boil for 1-2 minutes.
8. Add *sambhar* powder. Cook for ½ minute.
9. Add ginger-garlic paste. Cook for ½ minute.
10. Add the boiled *dal*. Add salt to taste. Boil for 5-6 minutes. Serve hot with vadas or other South Indian food.

Nugget Rolls

Servings 3 rolls

- Pancakes filled with vegetable and minced nuggets.

INGREDIENTS

for the filling

2 tbsp minced nutri nuggets (nutri granules)
1 onion - chopped finely
1 carrot - grated
½ cup shredded cabbage
½ tsp pepper
¼ tsp sugar - optional
salt to taste
4 tbsp oil

for the pancakes

½ cup *maida* (plain flour)
3/4 cup milk
¼ tsp salt
2 pinches *soda* (soda-bicarb).
oil for shallow frying

METHOD

for the filling

1. Soak nuggets for 15-20 minutes in warm water.
2. Cut cabbage into thin long strips (shred).
3. Heat 2½ tbsp oil. Add the drained nuggets and cook on slow fire for 1-2 minutes. Keep aside.
4. Heat 1½ tbsp oil. Add onions and cook for 1 minute.
5. Add cabbage and carrot and cook for ½ minute. Remove from fire.
6. Add the fried nuggets to the vegetables. Add salt and pepper to taste. Sugar may be added. Keep filling aside.

for the pancakes

1. Sift *maida*, salt and soda-bicarb.
2. Add milk gradually, beating well to make a smooth thin batter for pancakes.
3. Heat a non-stick pan, (not too hot).
4. Smear ½ tsp oil on it.
5. Remove from fire and pour 1 big *karchi* (¼ cup) of batter. Spread the batter by tilting the pan, to cover the bottom evenly. Return to fire.
6. Remove the pancake from the pan when the underside is cooked.
7. Do not cook the other side.
8. Cool the pancakes on a dry cloth.

Contd...

METHOD

to make the roll

1. Make a paste by dissolving 1 tsp of maida in 1 tbsp of water. Keep aside.
2. Place some filling on one end of the pancake which is nearest to you.
3. Fold the left side and then the right side.
4. Keeping the sides folded, roll upwards.
5. Seal the edge with the maida paste.
6. Shallow fry in hot oil in a nonstick pan. Drain on absorbent paper.
7. Serve hot with tomato sauce.

Breakfast Sweets

A few recipes for sweetmeats follow, which, along with fruits, tea and coffee, are served as accompaniments to the main breakfast items.

Meethi-Sukhi Seviyan

Servings 4

- A breakfast sweet.

INGREDIENTS

1 cup bambino vermicelli
½ cup sugar
2 tbsp *desi ghee*
8-10 almonds - cut into thin long pieces
1 tbsp *kishmish* (raisins)
2-3 *chhoti illaichi* (green cardamom) - skinned & crushed
2 cups water
50 gms *khoya* (dried whole milk) - optional

METHOD

1. Boil sugar, water and crushed *chhoti illaichi*. Remove from fire. Keep the sugar syrup aside.
2. Fry vermicelli in a karahi with *ghee* on slow fire till brown. Add *kishmish* and shredded almonds. Cook for a few seconds. Switch off the fire.
3. Add the sugar syrup. Boil. Keep covered on slow fire till the syrup is dry and the vermicelli is cooked.
4. Serve hot garnished with crumbled *khoya* & whole almonds.

Shahi Tukri

Servings 6

- A breakfast treat!

INGREDIENTS

4 slices bread
2 cups milk
½ cup sugar
5-6 *chhoti illaichi* (green cardamom) - skinned & crushed
a pinch of *kesar* (saffron)
75 gms *khoya* (dried whole milk)
4-5 almonds - cut into thin long pieces
4-5 *pista* (pistachio) - cut into thin long pieces
1 sliver leaf
ghee - enough to fry bread

METHOD

1. Remove the side crusts of bread. Cut each slice into 3 pieces.
2. Fry in ghee till golden brown. Keep aside.
3. Heat milk to which sugar, *illaichi* and *kesar* has been added. Boil. Remove from fire.
4. Dip 4-5 fried slices in the hot milk. Keep them soaked for a few seconds.
5. Remove slices from milk and arrange in a flat serving platter.
6. Repeat with the other slices.
7. Mash *khoya* and add to the left over milk.
8. Cook this milk till it thickens and turns into *rabri* (15-20 minutes).
9. Pour the hot rabri over the toasts.
10. Decorate with silver leaf.
11. Sprinkle shredded almonds & *pista*.
12. Serve warm or cold, according to the weather.

Note : Shahi Tukri may be served as a dessert too.

Manpasand Suji-ka-Halwa

Servings 4

- The peach coloured halwa is my favourite with puris.

INGREDIENTS

1 cup *suji* (semolina)
6 semi heaped tbsp of *desi ghee* or *vanaspati ghee*
1 cup sugar
2 cups milk
2 cups water
4 *chhoti illaichi* (green cardamoms) - skinned and crushed
1/8 tsp orange colour
8-10 *kishmish* (raisins)
1 tbsp *pista* - cut into thin long pieces
8-10 almonds - cut into thin long pieces
1 silver leaf

METHOD

1. Mix milk, water, *kishmish*, crushed *illaichi*, orange colour and sugar.
2. Boil. Remove from fire. Stir to dissolve the sugar. Keep aside.
3. Heat *ghee* in a *karahi*. Fry suji on low heat till it just changes its colour.
4. Add milk mixture, stirring continuously for 7-8 minutes till the *halwa* leaves the sides of the *karahi*.
5. Remove from fire.
6. Keep in a serving dish. Decorate with silver leaf, shredded almonds and *pista*.
7. Serve hot.

Fruit Filled Pancakes

Servings 4-5 pancakes

- The ideal sweet with a continental breakfast.

INGREDIENTS

for the filling

1 big apple
2 tbsp sugar
4 tbsp water
few drops of lemon juice
1 tbsp strawberry jam
1 tsp cornflour

for the pancakes

½ cup *maida* (plain flour)
1 cup milk
a pinch of salt
1 tsp powdered sugar

METHOD

for the filling

1. Peel apple. Cut into small, thin pieces.
2. Add sugar, water and lemon juice to apples.
3. Keep on slow fire for 1-2 minutes in a small pan.
4. Remove the apples from the syrup.
5. Mix cornflour with the reserved syrup to a smooth paste.
6. Add the jam also. Stir until boiling and boil till slightly thick.
7. Mix apple pieces. Remove from fire.

for the pancakes

1. Mix all ingredients to a smooth, thin batter with an electric beater.
2. In a non-stick pan, put 1 tsp of oil in the centre and spread it slightly.
3. Spread 1 *karchi* (¼ cup) of batter to make a small pancake.
4. Cook on slow fire, adding 1-2 tsp of *ghee* or butter on the sides of the pancake.
5. Turn it when the underside is done. Cook for 1 minute.
6. Remove from fire.
7. Spread some filling and roll up. Serve hot.

Note : Tinned pineapple may be used instead of apples.

Coffee or Tea-Time Snacks

Snacks form an essential part of our life style. Snacks may be prepared well in advance, but the baking and frying should be done at the time of serving. The fried snacks should always be removed on paper first and then transferred to the serving dish. To entertain guests with snacks, small cane baskets, lovely tiny bowls to serve tomato ketchup, smart snack trays and such knick-knacks really enable you to serve in style. In the absence of good snack trays you could just cover up a tray or a full plate with aluminium foil & serve your snacks on it. People get floored when things are done in style. Always keep paper napkins handy as quite a bit of our Indian snacks are greasy.

Date and Walnut Roll

Servings 10 pieces

- A winter delicacy!

INGREDIENTS

250 gms dates - deseeded and chopped
1 cup milk
1½ tbsp *malai or desi ghee*
½ cup walnuts - broken into bits
1 tbsp desiccated coconut

METHOD

1. Wash, clean dates. Remove seeds and chop them.
2. Pressure cook chopped dates with 1 cup milk. After the first whistle, keep on low heat for 15 minutes. Remove from fire.
3. When the pressure comes down, mash the dates. Add *ghee* or *malai* and cook till the dates stop sticking to the cooker.
4. Remove from the cooker and mix in the walnuts nicely.
5. Shape into a roll. Flatten the sides. Roll over desiccated coconut. Keep in the fridge in a container.
6. At the time of serving, cut into slices.

Bread Bhelpuri

Servings 4

- Spicy and delicious.

INGREDIENTS

3 slices bread
chaat masala to taste
1 small *kheera* (cucumber) - chopped finely
1 onion - chopped finely
2 green chillies - chopped finely
1 tbsp chopped coriander
50 gms - 1 cup *namkeen sev* (*Bikaneri bhujiya*)
1 cup fresh *annar ke dane* (pomegranate seeds) or
1 tomato - chopped finely
salt to taste
2 tbsp *imli* (tamarind) *ki chutney*
2 tbsp *poodina* (mint) *ki chutney*
oil for frying
lemon rings to serve

METHOD

1. Cut bread slices into tiny square pieces. Deep fry to a golden brown colour. Cool.
2. Mix fried bread cubes, onion, *annar*, *kheera*, *sev*, green chillies and chopped coriander.
3. Sprinkle some *chaat masala*.
4. Add *chutneys* to taste. Mix well.
5. Arrange one or two cabbage leaves in a bowl. Fill with the prepared bhelpuri and sprinkle some more *sev* and *annar*.
6. Serve immediately, garnished with lemon rings otherwise it tends to get soggy.

Paneer Pakora

Servings 10 pakoras

- The common pakoras made special!

INGREDIENTS

for the batter

1½ cups *besan* (gram flour)
2 pinches of *mitha soda* or baking powder
1 tsp salt
1 tsp red chilli powder
¼ tsp *ajwain* (carom seeds) - crushed
1 cup milk (approx)

for the filling

1¼ tsp salt
1½ tsp red chilli powder
1½ tsp *garam masala* (mixed spices)
1½ tsp *dhania* (coriander) powder
4-5 tsp lemon juice

Other ingredients

400 gms *paneer* (cottage cheese)
oil for deep frying

METHOD

1. Mix all the ingredients of the batter except milk.
2. Add enough milk gradually, to get a thick batter.
3. Beat the batter well.
4. Mix all ingredients of the filling to make a thick paste.
5. Cut *paneer* into slices which are slightly thicker than ¼".
6. Cut these slices into 1½" square pieces.
7. Slit the *paneer* piece half way, not till the end.
8. Insert a little filling in the slit with the help of a knife. Repeat with other *paneer* pieces.
9. If any filling is left over, apply it on the surface of the *paneer* pieces.
10. Heat oil. Dip *paneer* pieces in batter and deep fry on medium fire to a golden brown colour.
11. Serve hot with *poodina chutney* to which a little *imli ki chutney* is also mixed.

Kaathi-Kababs

Picture on facing page
Servings 8-10

- A filling snack. Ideal for high tea.

INGREDIENTS

to boil with the channas

1 cup *kale channe* (black gram)

1 tbsp *channe ki dal*
1 tsp *zeera* (cumin seeds)
1 stick *dalchini* (cinnamon)
3 *moti illaichi* (brown cardamoms)
3-4 *laung* (cloves)
3-4 *saboot kali mirch* (peppercorns)
1 tbsp *saboot dhania* (coriander seeds)
8-10 flakes garlic
1" piece ginger
3 dry, red whole chillies
1 onion - chopped

METHOD

for the kababs

1. Soak *channas* overnight.
2. Pressure cook with all the ingredients and just enough water (2 cups approx.) till done.
3. If there is any water left, dry the *channas* on fire.
4. Cool. Dry grind to a fine paste.
5. Add salt to taste.
6. Make flattened rounds of 1" diameter.
7. Shallow fry on a *tawa* on slow fire using 2-3 tbsp oil.

Contd...

1. Chocolate Log — Recipe on page 45
2. Kaathi Kabab — Recipe on page 42

for the rotis

1½ cups *maida* (plain flour)
1 tbsp oil
1 big potato - boiled and grated
3/4 tsp salt

for the rotis

1. Sift *maida* with salt. Add oil. Add grated potato, seeing that there are no lumps in it.
2. Knead to get a soft dough of rolling consistency using a little water.
3. Make thin roti on a *tawa*, without any oil.
4. Cook the roti on both sides on a hot *tawa*. Keep aside in a casserole.

to make kathi kababs

1. Mix one sliced onion in mint chutney or add a few drops of lemon juice to sliced onions with salt and red chilli powder.
2. Fry the roti lightly on one side only.
3. On the unfried side of the roti, put 2 kababs in the centre.
4. Put some onions on the kababs.
5. Fold the two sides of the roti to cover the kababs.
6. Fold the napkin into a triangle.
7. Wrap half the roti in a triangular piece of napkin.
8. Serve with spring onions cut into flowers as shown in the picture.

to make spring onion flowers

1. Cut the green part such that it is only about 2" long.
2. Slice off ¼" from the end of the white part.
3. Make slits on the white part, not too deep, but closely.
4. Leaving 1" space in the centre, between the white and green part, slit the greens also.
5. Dip in chilled water for an hour or more.
6. The onion opens up like a flower.

Chocolate Log

Servings 12 *Picture on page 42*

- Cake rolled up with chocolate cream & decorated with marzipan roses and leaves.

INGREDIENTS

for the cake

4 large eggs
10 level tbsp *maida* (plain flour)
10 level tbsp powdered sugar
1 tsp vanilla essence
2 level tsp baking powder
1 baking tray - size 9" x 11" approx.

METHOD

for the cake

1. Separate white and yolk of eggs.
2. Beat egg whites in a dry pan till stiff.
3. Add sugar gradually, beating after each addition. Add essence.
4. Sift *maida* with baking powder.
5. Add *maida* to the eggs and fold with a spoon.
6. Pour into a greased and dusted rectangular baking tray.
7. Bake for 15 minutes in a preheated oven at 200°C.
8. When the cake leaves the sides of the tray and is springy to touch, remove from the oven.
9. Spread powdered sugar on a grease proof paper or aluminium foil and turn out the cake over the sugar.
10. Spread half of the chocolate filling (recipe given on next page). Roll upwards with the help of the paper. Keep the left over chocolate filling in the freezer.
11. Pack the roll tightly in a polythene and keep aside for 15-20 minutes.
12. Cover the roll generously with the left over chocolate filling. Mark with a fork to give it a log appearance.
13. Decorate with marzipan roses. The recipe is given on the next page.

Contd...

for the chocolate filling

6 heaped tbsp (100 gms) white butter
1 cup icing sugar
1 tsp vanilla essence
3 tbsp cocoa powder

for the chocolate filling

1. Sift sugar & cocoa together.
2. In a small pan, put butter. Beat till slightly soft.
3. Add the sugar, cocoa and essence to the butter. Beat till light and fluffy.
4. More cocoa can be added for a darker colour.

Marzipan Roses

INGREDIENTS

2 tbsp almonds or cashewnuts
1½ tbsp icing sugar - sifted
½ tbsp cornflour
a few drops of water
green, yellow or red food color (liquid)

METHOD

to prepare marzipan paste

1. Soak almonds & remove skin. Grind blanched almonds or cashewnuts to a fine paste.
2. Add sifted sugar and cornflour to the paste.
3. Make a dough with a few drops of water.
4. Add yellow or red colour to 3/4 dough for the flowers and green colour to ¼ of the dough for the leaves. Cover the dough. Keep aside.

to make marzipan roses and leaves

1. Make a small ball about the size of a *kishmish* with the flower dough.
2. Flatten it by keeping it on the palm of your left hand and press with the other hand.
3. Roll to form the centre of the rose.
4. Take another small ball of the dough, flatten it and arrange besides the centre to form a petal. Make more petals similarly to complete the rose.
5. To make leaves, make a small elongated ball, press it to give the shape of a leaf. Mark lines with a knife on the leaf to give the impression of veins.

Chocolate Fudge

Servings 20 pieces

- For people with a sweet tooth!

INGREDIENTS

1½ cups sugar
1 cup milk
1 cup chopped walnuts
2½ tbsp cocoa
100 gms white butter (2/3 cup approx)
3-4 drops of vanilla essence

METHOD

1. Mix sugar, butter, milk and cocoa. Keep on low heat.
2. Cook stirring continuously for about 20 minutes, with a wooden spoon till the setting point is reached (when a drop of chocolate fudge sets into a ball when dropped in water). It attains a thick pouring consistency at this stage.
3. Remove from fire. Add chopped walnuts and essence. Turn into a greased plate with sides (thali).
4. When half-set mark into desired shape.

Spring Roll-Ups

Servings 12 pieces

- An interesting snack!

INGREDIENTS

for the pancake

5 tbsp *maida*
2 small eggs
¼ tsp salt
¼ tsp pepper
½ cup milk - approx.

for the filling

200 gms *paneer* (cottage cheese) - mashed
2 small capsicums - chopped finely
1 big onion - chopped finely
2 green chillies - chopped finely
½ tsp red chilli powder
½ tsp *garam masala*
salt to taste
1 tbsp oil

METHOD

for the pancake

1. Mix all ingredients to get a batter of a very thin pouring consistency.
2. Heat a non-stick pan. Smear 1 tsp oil in the centre.
3. Remove from fire and pour one *karchi* (1/3 cup) of batter. Spread by tilting the pan to cover the base. Cook on slow fire.
4. When the underside is cooked, remove from the pan to a plate.

for the filling

1. Cook onions and capsicum in oil till onions turn pink.
2. Add *paneer* and green chillies.
3. Add salt, red chilli powder and *garam masala*. Cook for 1 minute.
4. Remove from fire & cool.

to make the roll ups

1. Cut 1½" strip from two sides of the pancake. Keep the strips aside.
2. Cut the left over pancake into two equal pieces lengthwise.
3. Horizontally place the 1½" strip on the edge of one piece, across it.

Contd...

METHOD

4. Put 1 tbsp full of the filling in the centre of the horizontal strip.
5. Fold the sides of the strip to cover the filling.
6. Roll the piece of pancake tightly. Join the ends with a little maida paste. Keep aside.
7. Similarly prepare the second roll with the second piece of pancake.
8. Shallow fry in very little oil in a pan on low heat. Serve hot on a bed of open cabbage leaves and thickly sliced capsicums.

Note: Do not let the roll-ups turn brown on frying, so do not heat the oil to smoking point at the time of frying.

Special Apple Sandwich

Servings 6

- Very nutritive!

INGREDIENTS

6 slices of fresh bread (preferably sandwich bread)
cabbage, lettuce or *palak* (spinach) leaves - any green leaf

for the filling

1 apple
½ carrot
2 tbsp grated cucumber or cabbage
2 tbsp butter
1 tbsp fresh *malai* or 1 more tbsp butter
25 gm (1 cube) processed cheese - grated
1/8 tsp salt
¼ tsp pepper

METHOD

1. Soften butter. Add *malai* and cheese. Beat well.
2. Peel carrot, apple and *kheera*. Grate them and mix with the butter mixture, keep aside.
3. Boil 2 cups water with ½ tsp salt and ½ tsp sugar. Drop the green leaves into boiling water. Remove after 2-3 seconds. Dry the leaves.
4. Spread 1 heaped tbsp of filling on a slice of fresh bread.
5. Cover with a green leaf.
6. Butter the second slice lightly and place on the leaf. Press.
7. Cut the sides. Cut into two and serve on a bed of shredded carrots and cabbage.

Corn Fritters

Servings 15-20 pieces

- Enjoyable during the rainy days.

INGREDIENTS

4 whole corn cobs
2-3 green chillies
1 small bunch coriander
½ tsp red chilli powder
½ tsp *garam masala*
salt to taste
2-4 tbsp besan - enough to bind

METHOD

1. Grate corn cobs.
2. Add all other ingredients.
3. Heat oil - not to smoking point.
4. Drop a teaspoon full mixture at a time, dropping 10-12 teaspoons, to make fritters.
5. Fry on low heat till golden brown.
6. Serve with mint chutney.

Note: If the corn is hard, boil the whole corn and then grate it.

Moong Balls in Masala

Servings 20 balls.

- A light snack - not fried.

INGREDIENTS

for the balls

1 cup *dhuli moong dal* (split green beans)
1 tsp level salt
4 tbsp oil

for the masala

4-5 tbsp oil
3 onions
2 tomatoes
½" ginger piece - grated
2 green chillies - chopped
½ tsp salt
¼ tsp *garam masala*
¼ tsp chilli powder

METHOD

for the balls

1. Soak *dal* for 2 hours. Grind with minimum amount of water to a smooth paste.
2. Cook the *dal* in 4 tbsp of oil in a *karahi* for about 10 minutes on slow fire by sprinkling water occasionally.
3. Cook till *dal* is dry.
4. Make marble sized balls with greased hands. Keep aside.

for the masala

1. Heat oil.
2. Add onions. Cook till golden brown.
3. Add chopped tomatoes. Cook till oil separates.
4. Add ginger & green chillies.
5. Add all spices. Add 2-3 tbsp of water. Cook for 1 minute.
6. Add the balls. Mix well.
7. Serve sprinkled with chopped coriander.

Tikhat Sheera

- Hot'n spicy - a Maharashtrian snack.

INGREDIENTS

1 cup *suji* (semolina) - not very fine
1 onion - chopped finely
1 potato - chopped finely
2 green chillies - chopped finely
¼ cup shelled peas
or
tiny florets of cauliflower
6 tbsp oil
3/4 tsp *rai* (mustard seeds)
3-4 twigs curry leaves
1 tsp salt
½ tsp *haldi* (turmeric powder)
½ tsp red chilli powder
1 tomato - chopped finely

METHOD

1. Roast *suji* till slightly pink and starts smelling.
2. Heat oil. Add *rai* & curry leaves. Let them crackle for a few seconds.
3. Add onions. Cook till pink.
4. Add potatoes, peas or cauliflower and green chillies. Cook for 2-3 minutes.
5. Add *haldi* and red chilli powder.
6. Cook for a few seconds.
7. Add 2½ cups water. Add salt. Boil.
8. Slow down the fire and cook covered till vegetables are done.
9. Add *suji* gradually, stirring continuously. Mix well.
10. Add chopped tomatoes and cook for a few minutes.
11. Serve sprinkled with fresh coriander.

Cocktail Gobi Samosas

Servings 20

- Home made dainty samosas!

INGREDIENTS

for the dough

3/4 cup *maida* (plain flour)
¼ cup *suji* (semolina)
a pinch of baking powder
¼ tsp salt
2 semi heaped tbsp of *ghee* (vanasapati) or margarine

for the filling

1 medium cauliflower - grated
2 small boiled potatoes - mashed coarsely
¼" piece ginger - grated
½ tsp red chilli powder
salt to taste
3/4 tsp roasted *zeera* pd. (cumin seeds)
3/4 tsp *garam masala*
¼ tsp *amchoor* (dried mango powder)
1 tbsp broken cashewnuts
1 tbsp *kishmish* (raisins)
2 green chillies - finely chopped
¼ tsp sugar

METHOD

for the dough

1. Mix all ingredients.
2. Add a few tbsp of water and knead to form a stiff dough.
3. Keep covered for ½ hour.

for the filling

1. Heat 3 tbsp of oil. Put off the fire. Add ginger. Add salt, red chilli powder, *garam masala*, *zeera*, and *amchoor*. Return to fire.
2. Add nuts. Cook for a few seconds.
3. Add potatoes. Cook for ½ minute.
4. Add cauliflower. Mix well. Add sugar and green chillies.
5. Cover and cook on slow fire till the cauliflower is cooked. Make the filling spicy.

to prepare the samosas

1. Make marble sized balls of the dough.
2. Roll out thinly. Cut into two.
3. Fold each half into a triangle to form a cone.
4. Seal the cone by applying water. Fill 1 tbsp of the filling inside the cone.

Contd...

METHOD

5. Make a small fold or pleat on the side opposite to the joint of the cone.
6. Now close the cone with water. Press the side opposite to the pointed side against a plate, giving it a *samosa* look.
7. Heat oil. Deep fry 8-10 pieces at a time on low heat.

Sumptuous Meals

To make the party a success, the hostess should plan the menu a day or two in advance, so that there is enough time to shop properly. The important thing to keep in mind is that the dishes should differ in taste and colour. Take extra care to garnish each dish differently. Buffet parties being in vogue, too many gravies should be avoided as they are inconvenient to handle. I feel, if you have decided upon the dishes, and you are clear in your mind about what to cook, half your work for the party is over. Now the only work left, is to prepare these simple dishes which can be on the table in no time. So, get started!

Dishes With Gravy
Rassedar Sabziyan

Dal-Palak

Servings 6

- A nutritive combination of dal and spinach.

INGREDIENTS

½ cup *channe ki dal* (split gram)
½ kg *palak* (spinach)
2 tomatoes
1-2 green chillies - chopped
½" ginger - chopped
1 tsp coriander powder
½ tsp *garam masala* (mixed spices)
½ tsp red chilli powder
3 tbsp oil
1 onion - chopped

METHOD

1. Soak *dal* for ½ hour.
2. Wash, chop *palak* leaves. Discard the stems.
3. Heat oil in a pressure cooker. Fry onions till golden brown.
4. Strain the soaked *dal*. Add this *dal*, *palak* and all other ingredients, including the spices.
5. Add ¼ cup water.
6. Pressure cook to give 2 whistles, then cook on low heat for 8-10 minutes.
7. After the pressure comes down, mash the *dal* slightly.
8. Serve hot with boiled rice or chappatis.

Khoya Matar Makhana

Servings 4

- A rich dish, good for parties.

INGREDIENTS

1 cup shelled peas
100 gms *khoya* (dried whole milk)
1 cup *makhanas* (puffed lotus seeds)
3 tomatoes - pureed
2 big onions
1" piece ginger
2 green chillies
1 tbsp chopped coriander
1 tbsp *khus-khus* (poppy seeds)
1 tsp *dhania* (coriander powder)
½ tsp red chilli powder
½ tsp *garam masala* (mixed spices)
salt to taste
1 tbsp *kishmish* (raisins)

METHOD

1. Fry *makhanas* to a golden brown colour.
2. Grind onions, ginger, chillies & coriander leaves with a little water in a grinder to a paste.
3. Soak *khus-khus* for 10-15 minutes and grind to a smooth paste.
4. Heat 4 tbsp oil. Add the onion-ginger paste. Cook on low heat till oil separates.
5. Add the *khus-khus* paste. Cook for 1-2 minutes.
6. Add tomatoes pureed in a grinder. Cook till oil separates.
7. Add *dhania* powder, red chilli powder and *garam masala*.
8. Grate *khoya*. Add khoya and mix well for 1 minute.
9. Add peas and *makhanas*. Mix well.
10. Add *kishmish*.
11. Add enough water to get a thick gravy.
12. Cook covered till peas and *makhanas* are done.
13. Serve hot.

Panchratni Dal

Picture on facing page

Servings 4

- A fine blend of five dals.

INGREDIENTS

3 tbsp *urad dhuli dal*
3 tbsp *arhar dal*
3 tbsp *channe ki dal*
3 tbsp *moong dhuli dal*
3 tbsp *masoor dal*

for the baghar

4 tbsp oil
1 tsp *rai* (mustard seeds)
1 tsp *zeera* (cumin seeds)
2 *laung* (cloves)
½" stick *dalchini*
few curry leaves
2 dry red chillies - broken
2 green chillies - chopped
½" ginger piece - chopped
3 tomatoes - chopped
½ tsp *garam masala*
1 tbsp chopped coriander
juice of ½ lemon

METHOD

1. Clean, wash *dals*. Pressure cook *dals* together with 3½ cups of water and 1½ tsp of salt approx.
2. After the first whistle, keep on low heat for 5-7 minutes.

for the baghar (tempering)

1. Collect mustard seeds, *zeera*, *dalchini* and *laung* together.
2. Heat oil. Add the collected *zeera* etc. Cook for a few seconds.
3. Add the ginger, curry leaves, red and green chillies. Fry for a few seconds.
4. Add the tomatoes and *garam masala* and cook for 1-2 minutes.
5. Add this oil to the *dal*. Add coriander also.
6. Bring *dal* to boil, keep on slow fire for 2-3 minutes.
7. Add lemon juice. Mix well.
8. Serve hot.

1. Gobi Mussalam — Recipe on page 86
2. Methi wale Paranthe — Recipe on page 105
3. Panchratni Dal — Recipe on page 60

Benarsi Bharvan Aloo

Servings 4

- Potatoes stuffed with a delicious filling, served with a rich gravy.

INGREDIENTS

for the potatoes

4 large potatoes
2 tbsp *maida* (plain flour)
oil for frying

for the filling

100 gms *paneer* (cottage cheese)
1 small onion - finely chopped
½ cup boiled peas
2 tsp broken *kaju* (cashewnuts)
1 tsp *kishmish* (raisins)
1 green chilli - chopped finely
2 tbsp oil
salt to taste

METHOD

to prepare the potatoes

1. Peel, wash potatoes. Prick with a fork. Cut into two pieces.
2. Scoop out the inner portion.
3. Keep the potatoes in salted water and prepare the filling in the meantime. Keep aside.
4. Mix 2-3 tbsp water with maida to make a thick paste.

for the filling

1. Heat oil. Add onion and green chilli. Cook till onion turns light pink.
2. Add boiled peas, *kaju* & *kishmish*. Cook for 1 minute.
3. Add crumbled *paneer* and salt. Cook for a few seconds. Remove from fire and cool.

to fill the potatoes

1. Dry the cut potatoes.
2. Fill the potatoes with the prepared filling.
3. Join the two halves with *maida* paste and tooth picks.
4. Deep fry the prepared potatoes in medium hot oil. Keep aside.

Contd...

INGREDIENTS

for the gravy

4 tbsp oil
2 onions
½" piece ginger
¼ tsp *haldi* (turmeric powder)
½ tsp *garam masala* (mixed spices)
½ tsp red chilli powder
1 tsp *dhania* (coriander) powder
¼ cup beaten curd
2 tomatoes
50 gm *khoya* (dried whole milk)
salt to taste

METHOD

for the gravy

1. Grind onions & ginger.
2. Grind tomatoes separately.
3. Cook onion paste in oil on low heat till light brown.
4. Add *haldi*, coriander powder, and red chilli powder.
5. Add tomatoes and curd and cook till oil separates.
6. Slow down the fire and mix in the *khoya*. Cook for a few seconds.
7. Add salt to taste.
8. Add the fried potatoes and enough water to get a thick gravy.
9. Cook covered till the potatoes are tender.

Methi Malai Matar

Picture on page 2

Servings 4

- Enjoy the subtle methi flavour even in summers!

INGREDIENTS

1½ cups shelled, boiled peas
½ stick *dalchini* (cinnamon)
2 *moti illaichi* (cardamom)
3-4 *laung* (cloves)
2 tbsp cashewnuts
2 tbsp oil
1 onion - grated
¼ tsp white pepper powder
½ cup (75 gms) *malai* or cream
4 tbsp *kasoori methi* (dry fenugreek leaves)
salt to taste
½ tsp red chilli powder
a pinch of sugar
½ cup milk (approx)

METHOD

1. Boil peas in salted water till tender.
2. Grind together *dalchini*, *laung* and seeds of *moti illaichi* on a *chakla-belan*. Keep aside.
3. Grind cashewnuts separately with a little water to a paste.
4. Heat oil. Add grated onion and cook on low heat till oil separates. Do not let the onions turn brown.
5. Add the freshly ground *masala* and pepper powder. Cook for a few seconds.
6. Add the *kasoori methi* and *malai*, cook on low heat for 2-3 minutes till *malai* dries up.
7. Add the boiled peas.
8. Add cashewnut paste and cook for a few seconds.
9. Add enough milk to get a thick gravy.
10. Add salt, sugar to taste & red chilli powder.
11. Serve garnished with peas in the centre surrounded by a ring of cashewnut bits.

Channa aur Dhingri Curry

Servings 6

- An interesting dish to prepare when you find it difficult to decide a fresh vegetable.

INGREDIENTS

125 gms (1 cup approx.) *kabuli channe* (bengal gram)
1 cup *dhingri* (white dry mushrooms)
4 onions
10-15 flakes garlic - optional
1" piece ginger
4 tomatoes
½ tsp *haldi* (turmeric)
½ tsp red chilli powder
2 tsp *dhania* (coriander) powder
½ tsp *garam masala* (mixed spices)
½ tsp black pepper
salt to taste
5 tbsp *ghee* or oil

METHOD

1. Soak *dhingri* and *channas* separately overnight.
2. Cut *dhingri* into small pieces.
3. Pressure cook *channas* with salt till tender.
4. Grind ginger, garlic and onions to a paste.
5. Grind tomatoes to a puree.
6. Heat ghee. Fry onions till light brown.
7. Add tomato puree. Cook till *ghee* separates.
8. Add *haldi*, *dhania* powder, and red chilli powder. Cook for a few seconds.
9. Strain the *channas* reserving the water. Add the *channas* and *dhingri*. Cook on slow fire for a few minutes.
10. Add the *channa* water. Simmer for 10-15 minutes. Add salt, black pepper and garam masala.
11. Serve hot, sprinkled with chopped coriander leaves.

Paneer Makhani

Picture on facing page *Servings 4*

- Cottage cheese in tomato gravy with a tangy flavour.

INGREDIENTS

250 gm *paneer* (cottage cheese) - ½" thick pieces of 1" x 1"
3 tbsp butter or *ghee*
400 gms (7-8 medium) tomatoes - chopped
½" piece ginger - chopped
1 *tej patta* (bay leaf)
2 *moti illaichi* (brown cardamoms) - skinned & crushed
1 tsp *kasoori methi* (dry fenugreek leaves)
½ tsp chilli powder
salt to taste (1 tsp approx)
1 tsp or slightly more sugar
¼ tsp *garam masala* (mixed spices)
5 tbsp (75 gm) cream or well beaten *malai*

METHOD

1. Heat *ghee* or butter in a *karahi*. Add tomatoes, ginger, *tej patta*, *moti illaichi*, *kasoori methi* and chilli powder.
2. Cook covered for about 10 minutes, till the tomatoes are pulpy.
3. Cool. Grind the tomatoes to a puree in the mixer.
4. Pass the puree through a fine sieve.
5. Keep the strained puree on fire. Add salt, *garam masala* and sugar to reduce the sour flavour.
6. Add 4 tbsp of cream. Remove from fire.
7. Add *paneer* pieces, about 1 hour before serving.
8. Garnish with swirls of beaten cream (1 tbsp) and slit green chillies tossed in oil.

1. Paneer Makhani — Recipe on page 66
2. Vegetable Biryani — Recipe on page 104

Kofta Rangeen

Picture on page 95 *Servings 8*

- The colourful koftas add colour to food.

INGREDIENTS

for the kofta filling
1 carrot - shredded on the grater
1 capsicum - shredded
3-4 tbsp shredded cabbage
1 small onion - shredded
1 tbsp oil
salt, pepper to taste

for the kofta covering
150 gms *paneer* (cottage cheese)
2 potatoes - boiled & grated
3 tbsp *maida* (plain flour)
½ tsp salt
¼ tsp *garam masala* (mixed spices)
¼ tsp red chilli powder
1 bread slice - squeezed out of water

METHOD

for the kofta filling
1. Shred all vegetables into thin long strips.
2. Heat oil in a *karahi*. Add onions. Cook for a few seconds.
3. Add capsicum. Fry for a few seconds.
4. Add cabbage & carrot. Stir fry for 1 minute.
5. Add salt and pepper to taste.
6. Remove from fire, cool.

for the kofta covering
1. Sift *maida*. Grate *paneer*.
2. Mix grated *paneer*, *maida* and other ingredients with the palm of the hand till the grains of the *paneer* disappear.
3. Divide into 4 big balls.
4. Flatten each ball to a size of about 2½" diameter.
5. Place 1 tbsp of filling in the centre.
6. Lift the sides to cover the filling.
7. Give the *kofta* an oval shape like an egg.
8. Roll in *maida* and deep fry *koftas* carefully to a golden brown colour.

Contd...

INGREDIENTS

for the gravy

4 tbsp oil
2 onions
2 *moti illaichi* (brown cardamom)
½" piece ginger
3/4 cup milk
3 tomatoes
1 tbsp tomato ketchup
1½ tsp *dhania* powder (coriander powder)
½ tsp red chilli powder
½ tsp *garam masala* (mixed spices)
salt to taste

METHOD

to prepare the gravy

1. Grind onions, ginger and seeds of moti illaichi together.
2. Grind tomatoes to a puree. Keep aside.
3. Heat oil. Add onion paste and cook on low heat till golden brown in colour.
4. Add *dhania* powder. Mix.
5. Add milk gradually, 2-3 tbsp at a time, stirring continuously till all the milk is used.
6. Cook on slow fire till the mixture turns brown again and the oil separates. Add red chilli powder.
7. Add the tomato puree, cook till oil separates.
8. Add enough water to get a thick gravy. Add salt, *garam masala*, and tomato ketchup and cook covered on slow fire for 5-7 minutes after the first boil. Keep aside.

to serve koftas

1. Cut koftas into two, lengthwise. Heat in a preheated oven for 3-4 minutes.
2. Boil the gravy separately, and pour in a serving dish.
3. Arrange the heated koftas on the gravy.
4. Serve immediately.

Hussaini Curry

Servings 4

- Masala vegetables arranged on toothpicks & served with a spicy gravy.

INGREDIENTS

1 big potato
5-6 french beans
2-3 carrots
few toothpicks
3 tbsp oil

for dry masala

2 tsp *saboot dhania* (coriander powder)
1½ tsp *zeera* (cumin seeds)
1 tsp red chilli powder
½ tsp *haldi* (turmeric powder)
6 *laung* (cloves)
5 *moti illaichi* (brown cardamom)

for the gravy

2 tsp dry masala - prepared as given above
2 onions
½" piece ginger - chopped
3-4 tbsp oil

METHOD

1. Grind all ingredients of the dry masala together. Keep aside.
2. Peel potatoes and carrots. String french beans.
3. Cut potatoes into ½" pieces, carrots into ¼" thick rounds and french beans into ½" long pieces.
4. Boil 2 cups of water with ½ tsp salt. Add the vegetables. Boil for about 5 minutes till cooked.
5. Strain, reserve the water for the gravy.
6. Heat 2 tbsp oil. Keeping aside 2 tsp of the ground dry masala, add the rest.
7. Immediately add the vegetables and ¼ tsp salt. Toss in masala for 2-3 minutes.
8. Cool the vegetables.
9. On a toothpick, pass a piece of potato, then french bean and lastly a round piece of carrot.
10. Make many such toothpicks and keep aside in an oven proof dish.

for the gravy

1. Grind chopped ginger and onion to paste.
2. Heat oil. Add *hing*. Add the ground dry masala.
3. Add the onion paste, cook till light brown and oil separates.

Contd...

INGREDIENTS	METHOD

a pinch of *hing* (asafoetida)
2 tomatoes - chopped
½ tsp *garam masala* (mixed spices)
salt to taste
water - kept aside of the boiled vegetables
½ tsp shredded ginger
¼ tsp *amchoor* (dried mango powder)

4. Add chopped tomatoes. Cook and mash till oil separates.
5. Add shredded ginger.
6. Add sufficient water of the boiled vegetables to get a thick gravy.
7. Add salt to taste, *garam masala* and *amchoor*.
8. Simmer on low heat for 5-7 minutes.

to serve

1. Heat the prepared toothpicks in a hot oven for 2-3 minutes.
2. Pour hot gravy on top and serve immediately.

Mughlai Paneer

Servings 6

- Really delicious!

INGREDIENTS

for the gravy

½ kg (6 big) onions - sliced finely
10-12 *kaju* (cashewnuts)
1 tbsp *khus-khus* (poppy seeds)
¼ cup fresh curd
2 tomatoes - blanched
½ cup milk
½ cup water (approx)
4 tbsp and 2 tbsp oil
1 tsp salt (to taste)
3/4 tsp red chilli powder
¼ tsp *garam masala* (mixed spices)

Other Ingredients

400 gms *paneer* (cottage cheese)
oil for deep frying

METHOD

1. Cut *paneer* into rectangular pieces of about ¼" thickness.
2. Heat oil and deep fry the *paneer* to a light colour. Keep aside.
3. Soak *kaju* and *khus-khus* in 2-3 tbsp hot water for 15 minutes.
4. Heat 4 tbsp oil and fry onions till they turn golden brown.
5. Remove from fire. Grind the onions to a wet brown paste with ¼ cup water.
6. Grind the soaked *kaju* and *khus-khus* to a wet white paste.
7. Heat 2 tbsp oil. Add the brownish onion paste and cook on low heat till golden brown.
8. Add beaten curd and cook till the paste turns brown again. (3-4 minutes).
9. Put the tomatoes in boiling water for 2 minutes. Remove from water and peel the skin to blanch them.
10. Add the blanched, chopped tomatoes. Cook till oil separates. Keep mashing while cooking.
11. Add *kaju* paste and cook on low heat for 3-4 minutes.
12. Add milk. Cook for 1-2 minutes. Add enough water to get a thick gravy. Add salt, pepper, red chilli powder & *garam masala*. Boil the gravy and simmer for 5-7 minutes till oil separates. Add the fried *paneer*. Serve hot.

Paneer Butter Masala

Servings 4-5

- Sheer delight!

INGREDIENTS

for the masala gravy

2 onions
1" piece ginger
6-7 flakes garlic
½ cup milk (100 ml)
4 big (250 gms) tomatoes
3 tbsp *ghee* or 5 tbsp oil
2 tbsp *kaju* (cashew nuts) - ground to a paste
2 tsp *kasoori methi* (dry fenugreek leaves)
3/4 tsp roasted *zeera* (cumin seeds) powder
1 tsp red chilli powder
1½ tsp salt - to taste
½ tsp *garam masala* (mixed spices)
¼ - ½ tsp sugar

Other Ingredients

250 gms *paneer* (cottage cheese) - cut into big cubes
1 green chilli - slit length wise
1 big capsicum - cut into thin rings
2 onions - cut into thin rings
2 tbsp salted butter
few drop orange colour

METHOD

1. Grind onions, ginger & garlic together.
2. Chop tomatoes roughly and grind them to a puree in a mixer.
3. Cook onions in *ghee*, till light brown and *ghee* separates. Do not make them dark brown. Add red chilli powder. Cook for ½ minute.
4. Add milk gradually. Cook for 2-3 minutes till ghee separates again.
5. Add *kaju* paste. Cook for 2-3 minutes.
6. Add tomatoes. Cook for 8-10 minutes on slow fire till *ghee* separates. Add *bhuna zeera powder*, *garam masala*, salt and sugar.
7. Add enough water, about 1½ cups. Cook on low heat for another 10-12 minutes till the *ghee* separates and the gravy dries up to a thick masala gravy.
8. Add *kasoori methi*. Keep aside.
9. Heat butter in a clean *karahi*, add green chillies, capsicum and onions.
10. Saute for 2-3 minutes.
11. Add these vegetables to the prepared gravy.
12. Add *paneer* also.
13. Add colour. Keep on fire for 2-3 minutes.
14. Serve hot with nans or tandoori paranthas.

Note : For the recipe of nans and tandoori parantha, refer to my book - "Vegetarian Wonders".

Shahi Kaaju Aloo

Picture on page 1 *Servings 8-10*

- Potatoes are simmered in a delicious, white gravy. Curd and cashews form the base of this royal (shahi) curry. Black cumin lends it's royal flavour to the humble potatoes.

INGREDIENTS

300 gm (4) potatoes
2 tbsp cahews - soaked in ¼ cup water
1 tbsp chopped ginger
1 tsp chopped garlic
½ tsp shah jeera (black cumin)
1 tej patta (bay leaf)
2 onions - chopped
a pinch of haldi
¼ tsp garam masala
2 tbsp chopped coriander
¼ cup curd - whisked to make it smooth
¼ cup milk
4 tbsp oil for frying

METHOD

1. Wash potatoes and peel. Cut potatoes into 1" pieces.
2. Fry the potatoes to a deep golden brown and keep aside.
3. Grind cashews, ginger and garlic to a paste in a small coffee or spice grinder. Keep the cashew paste aside.
4. Heat 4 tbsp oil in a heavy bottomed pan. Add shah jeera and tej patta. Wait for 30 seconds till jeera stops spluttering.
5. Add onions and cook till they turn soft but do not let them turn brown. Add *haldi* and garam masala. Stir to mix well.
6. Add cashew paste. Cook for 1 minute. Add curd and stir fry on low heat till water evaporates. Cook till dry.
7. Add milk and about ½ cup water to get a gravy. Boil and simmer for 2-3 minutes.
8. Add the fried potatoes and chopped coriander to the gravy and simmer on low heat.
9. Cook on low heat till the gravy gets thick and coats the potatoes. Serve hot with *rotis* or *paranthas*.

Dry Dishes
Sukhi Sabziyan

Achaari Aloo

Picture on facing page
Servings 5-6

- Pickle flavoured potatoes.

INGREDIENTS

½ kg baby potatoes
2 tsp *saunf* (aniseeds)
1 tsp *rai* (mustard seeds)
a pinch of *methi dana* (fenugreek seeds)
½ tbsp *kalonji* (onion seeds)
1 tbsp *zeera* (cumin seeds)
5-6 flakes garlic-optional
3 tbsp broken *kaju* (cashewnuts)
½ cup curd
4-5 tbsp oil
2 onions - sliced finely
3-4 green chillies - chopped
1 tsp *haldi* (turmeric) powder
1 tsp *amchoor* (dried mango powder
2-3 green chillies-slit
salt to taste

METHOD

1. Peel potatoes. Boil in salted water till they get cooked properly.
2. Collect *saunf*, mustard seeds, *methi dana*, *kalonji*, and *zeera* together.
3. Crush garlic roughly and keep aside.
4. Grind *kaju*. Mix curd in it and keep aside.
5. Heat oil. Add the collected seeds together. Let them crackle.
6. Add garlic. Saute for a few seconds. Add onions and chopped chillies. Cook till onions turn golden brown.
7. Add *haldi*. Mix.
8. Add the boiled potatoes. Cook for 5 minutes.
9. Add the *kaju-curd* mixture gradually and keep stirring. Add *amchoor* and salt if required. Cook covered for some time. Keep aside.
10. At the time of serving, add the slit green chillies and heat the potatoes.
11. Serve hot, decorated with a tomato flower and sprigs of coriander.

to make a tomato flower

1. Peel a long, ½" broad strip of the tomato peel, all around the whole tomato.
2. Roll the strip to make a flower.

1. Achaari Aloo — Recipe on page 76
2. Paneer Tawa Masala — Recipe on page 85

Hyderabadi Baingan

Servings 8

- The ultimate experience of brinjals!

INGREDIENTS

500 gm *baingan* (brinjals)- small round variety
6-7 flakes garlic - optional
1" piece of ginger
5-6 tomatoes - chopped finely
1 lemon sized ball of *imli* (tamarind)
6 tsp coriander powder
½ tsp red chilli powder
salt to taste
1-2 tbsp sugar
5-6 tbsp oil

METHOD

1. Wash *baingans*. Give two cross cuts (slits) till half the way, starting from the top.
2. Grind ginger and garlic together.
3. Soak *imli* in ½ cup hot water. Mash well and take out the juice.
4. Heat oil. Add garlic-ginger paste. Cook for 1-2 minutes.
5. Add tomatoes. Cook till oil separates.
6. Add chilli powder and coriander powder. Cook for a few seconds.
7. Add sugar and *imli* juice.
8. Add the *baingans*.
9. Cook covered till done, adding a little water occasionally.
10. Serve hot.

Benarsi Gobi

Servings 4-5

- Cauliflower coated with a special masala.

INGREDIENTS

½ kg cauliflower
3-4 green chillies
3-4 tbsp chopped coriander
1 tsp *zeera* (cumin seeds)
½ tsp salt
1" piece ginger
3 big onions - finely chopped
2 tbsp oil
¼ tsp *haldi* (turmeric powder)
½ cup curd - beaten
¼ cup *malai* (cream) - optional
oil for frying

METHOD

1. Cut cauliflower into big florets, with a little stem.
2. Deep fry to a light colour. Do not let them turn brown.
3. Grind green chillies, coriander, salt, *zeera* and ginger to a paste.
4. Rub the coriander paste over and inside the fried pieces of cauliflower. Keep aside.
5. Heat oil. Add onions. Cook till transparent. Add *haldi* powder.
6. Add curd and *malai. Cook for a few minutes.*
7. Add cauliflower. Toss for a few seconds till the masala coats the cauliflower.
8. Serve hot.

Dal Maharani

Servings 4

- The radish & it's green leaves impart a special taste and appearance to the dal.

INGREDIENTS

for boiling with the dal

1 cup *urad dhuli dal* (split black beans) - soaked for 30 minutes
1" piece ginger - very finely chopped
4-5 flakes garlic - very finely chopped
2 green chillies - very finely chopped
½ tsp *haldi* (turmeric) powder
1¼ tsp salt
1 cup water

for the baghar (tempering)

1 big onion - finely chopped
1 big tomato - finely chopped
½ *mooli* (radish) with tender leaves
chopped leaves of one radish (5-6 leaves)
½ tsp *garam masala* (mixed spices)
½ tsp chilli power
2 tbsp *ghee* or oil

METHOD

1. Clean, wash *dal*. Soak *dal* in water for ½ hour.
2. Strain *dal*.
3. Pressure cook *dal* with 1 cup water and all other ingredients. When the first whistle comes, slow down the fire & keep for 1 minute only.
4. Remove from fire. Open the cooker only after the pressure drops down.

for the baghar (tempering)

1. Cut radish leaves into thin long strips.
2. Heat *ghee* or oil. Add onions. Cook till brown. Add tomatoes. Cook for 2-3 minutes.
3. Add chopped radish. Cook for 1 minute.
4. Add leaves. Mix. Add ½ tsp chilli powder and ½ tsp *garam masala*.
5. Pour into the *dal*. Mix gently.
6. Serve with finely cut onion rings made pink and crisp by mixing with beetroot shreds and keeping them together in chilled water for sometime.

Lazeez Miloni

Servings 4 — *Picture on cover*

INGREDIENTS

4 small onions - cut into 4 pieces and separated
2 capsicums (green, yellow or red) - cut into 8 pieces
2 carrots - cut into diagonal slices
10-12 french beans - cut into 2" long pieces diagonally
1 tbsp ginger - shredded
1 tsp lemon juice
25 gm *paneer* (cottage cheese), optional
3 tbsp oil
1½ tsp salt
1 tsp *dhania* (coriander) powder
½ tsp red chilli powder
1/3 cup cream or malai beaten with some cold milk
½ tsp *garam masala*

for the paste
1 green chilli
1" piece ginger
1 tbsp chopped coriander
1 tsp *zeera* (cumin seeds)
3-4 *saboot kali mirch* (pepper corns)

METHOD

1. Peel carrots. Cut into diagonal slices.
2. Cut beans into long pieces with slanting ends.
3. Boil 3 cups water with 1 tsp salt. Add beans and carrots. As soon as the boil returns, remove from fire. Strain and refresh with cold water. Wipe dry on a clean kitchen towel.
4. Cut capsicum into 8 pieces.
5. Grind all ingredients of the paste together with a little water.
6. Heat oil. Add onions. Cook till golden.
7. Add carrots and beans. Stir for 2-3 minutes.
8. Add the ground paste. Cook for 1 minute. Add shredded ginger.
9. Add capsicums.
10. Add salt, *dhania powder, garam masala* and red chilli powder. Mix well.
11. Add 1/3 cup cream or *malai*. Cook for 2-3 minutes.
12. Sprinkle lemon juice. Transfer the hot vegetables to a serving dish.
13. Garnish by grating *paneer* very finely, directly over the vegetables in the serving dish.

Tandoori Arbi

Picture on facing page *Servings 4*

- Try this different way of preparing arbi!

INGREDIENTS

½ kg *arbi* (calocasia) - medium size
1 cup curd of full cream milk - hung for 30 minutes
1 tbsp *tandoori masala*
1 tsp ginger paste
6-8 peppercorns - crushed
a pinch of haldi for colour
1 tbsp *besan*
4-5 onions - cut into rings
½" piece ginger - shredded
1½ tsp crushed *saboot dhania* (coriander seeds)
½ tsp *garam masala* (mixed spices)
4-5 tbsp oil
1½ tsp *amchoor* (dried mango powder)
3-4 green chillies - slit lengthwise
¼ tsp salt, or to taste
½ tsp *ajwain* (carom seeds)

METHOD

1. Hang curd in a muslin cloth for ½ hour.
2. Boil *arbi* in salted water with ½ tsp of *amchoor*, till soft. Peel and flatten the pieces.
3. Mix *tandoori masala*, ginger paste and crushed saboot kali mirch to hung curd. Add a pinch of *haldi* for colour. Add ½ tsp salt and *besan*.
4. Grease a wire rack. Dip *arbi* pieces in the prepared curd and arrange on the rack.
5. Keep in a hot oven for ½ hour. Grill a tray beneath till the curd dries up and forms a coating & *arbi* turns brownish. Keep arbi aside.
6. Heat oil. Add onions rings. Cook till light brown.
7. Add all spices and salt. Add the *arbi*.
8. Add the shredded ginger & green chillies. Mix well. Stir fry for 3-4 minutes.
9. Remove from fire. Serve hot.

Kadhahi Paneer

Picture on page 2
Servings 6

- Makes the table look beautiful & pleases the palate too!

INGREDIENTS

250 gms *paneer* (cottage cheese) - cut into long fingers
2 capsicums - cut into long fingers
2 dry red chillies
1½ tsp *saboot dhania* (coriander seeds)
1½" piece ginger - chopped finely
1" piece ginger - finely shredded
10-12 flakes garlic - crushed
1 green chilli - chopped
2 tomatoes - chopped
a pinch of *methi dana* (fenugreek seeds)
1 tbsp - chopped coriander
½ tsp salt
4 tbsp oil

METHOD

1. Heat red chillies on a *tawa*, till slightly crisp and dry.
2. Pound (crush roughly) red chillies and *saboot dhania* to a rough paste.
3. Heat 1 tbsp oil in a non-stick pan. Saute capsicums till done. Keep aside.
4. Heat 2 tbsp oil. Reduce flame. Add *methi dana*. Let it turn brown. Add crushed garlic. Fry till light brown.
5. Add pounded *dhania* & red chillies. Cook for ½ minute.
6. Add chopped ginger and green chilli.
7. Add tomatoes, stir fry till oil separates, about 5-7 minutes.
8. Add *paneer* & capsicum. Cook for 2-3 minutes.
9. Add shredded ginger and coriander. Mix well. Serve hot.

Note: You may roughly grind extra red chillies and coriander seeds in a coffee grinder and store it in an air tight bottle for future use.

Paneer Tawa Masala

Servings 4 *Picture on page 77*

- A colourful low calorie paneer dish!

INGREDIENTS

300 gms *paneer* (cottage cheese) slab - cut into ½" thick rectangle of size - 8"x3" approx. (get the *paneer* block cut horizontally when purchasing *paneer*)
2 capsicums
2 onions
1 firm tomato
1 cup (200 gms) curd of full cream milk
¾ tsp salt
½ tsp red chilli powder
¼ tsp orange red colour

for the dry masala powder

Grind together coarsely
5-6 *chhoti illaichi* (green cardamom)
3-4 sticks *dalchini* (cinnamon)
8-10 *laung* (cloves)
1 tsp *ajwain* (omum)
The excess can be stored in an airtight container.

METHOD

1. Hang the curd in a muslin cloth for 15 minutes.
2. Add salt, chilli powder and colour to curd.
3. Cover the *paneer* slab with this curd and place in a greased dish or on a greased rack for at least 15-20 minutes to marinate.
4. Keep the paneer in a preheated oven for 10-15 minutes or till the curd dries up and forms a coating. Turn the *paneer* block carefully.
5. Keep it in the oven for 5-7 minutes more.
6. Remove from the oven and keep aside.
7. Cut each capsicum into 8 pieces to get 1" pieces of capsicum. Cut each onion into four pieces and separate the onion leaves. Cut tomatoes into 8 pieces. Remove pulp.
8. Heat 1½ tbsp oil in a non-stick pan. Add 1 tsp of the prepared dry masala powder.
9. Immediately put the slab of *paneer*. Cook on low heat for 1 minute. Do not let it turn black.
10. Turn the slab again. Remove from pan.
11. At the time of serving, keep the *paneer* in a hot oven for 8-10 minutes till it gets soft.
12. In the meantime, heat 2 tbsp oil, add 1 tsp dry masala powder, add the capsicum & onions immediately. Cook for 2-3 minutes. Add tomatoes, sprinkle ½ tsp salt on the vegetables. Mix.
13. Serve these vegetables around the heated *paneer* kept in a flat serving dish.
14. Cut the *paneer* slab diagonally, 1" apart, and then give a cross cut, keeping the slab together.

Gobi Musallam

Picture on page 61

Servings 4-5

- Whole cauliflower steamed and then baked.

INGREDIENTS

for steaming

1 cauliflower - medium size
2 green chillies
1" piece ginger
½ tsp *garam masala*
½ tsp red chilli powder
3/4 tsp salt
1 tsp lemon juice

for the masala

2 onions
½" piece ginger
2 tomatoes
2 green chillies
3 tbsp oil
¼ cup curd - beaten
1 tsp *dhania* (coriander) powder

METHOD

1. Cut the stem of the cauliflower. Wash. Dry.
2. Grind ginger & green chillies to a paste. Add red chilli powder, *garam masala*, salt and lemon juice.
3. Insert this paste nicely between the florets.
4. Steam the cauliflower in an upright position by putting the stem part in a *katori* (small bowl) and placing it in a pressure cooker which has a little water at the bottom.
5. Cook the cauliflower, by pressure cooking till the hissing sound. Remove from fire before the first whistle.
6. In a *karahi* put 3-4 tbsp oil. Toss the steamed cauliflower, turning it carefully till it looks slightly fried and brownish in colour.

for the masala

1. Grind the tomatoes & green chillies together to a puree in a grinder.
2. Grind onions and ginger to a paste.
3. Cook onion paste in oil on low heat till onions turn brown and oil separates.
4. Add chilli powder and *dhania* powder. Cook for ½ minute.

Contd...

INGREDIENTS

salt & red chilli powder to taste
½ tsp *garam masala* (mixed spices)
½ cup boiled peas

METHOD

5. Add curd gradually. Cook for 3-4 minutes, till oil separates.
6. Add tomatoes. Cook for 8-10 minutes till oil separates.
7. Add boiled peas. Cook for 2-3 minutes.
8. Add just enough water (3-4 tbsp) to get a thick masala gravy. Add salt to taste. Keep on fire for a few minutes. Add *garam masala*.
9. Before serving, put the gravy on the cauliflower and bake in an oven for 15-20 minutes, till the cauliflower gets well done.

Note : **The cauliflower should not get over cooked while steaming. If the whistle happens to come, remove pressure by putting a little water on the lid of the cooker.**

Balti Aloo

Picture of facing page

Servings 4

- A perfect combination of five seeds are popped into hot oil to impart all their flavour. Fresh coriander leaves enhance the taste and look of this humble potato dish.

INGREDIENTS

4 medium potatoes
2 medium onions - sliced
3 tbsp oil
½ tsp *jeera* (cumin seeds)
½ tsp *saunf* (fennel seeds)
¼ tsp *kalonji* (nigella seeds)
¼ tsp *rai* (mustard seeds)
2 pinches of *methi dana* (fenugreek seeds)
4-6 flakes garlic - crushed
1" piece ginger - cut into match sticks
½ tsp *haldi*
1-2 dry, red chillies
a few curry leaves or fresh coriander leaves
salt to taste
1 tsp chat masala

METHOD

1. Peel, wash and cut potatoes into ¼" thick, round slices.
2. Heat oil in a non stick wok or a kadhai. Reduce heat, collect all seeds – *jeera, saunf, kalonji, rai* and *methi daana,* and add all together to the oil. Cook for ½ minute till the saunf starts changing colour.
3. Add garlic and ginger, stir fry for 1 minute.
4. Add onions, stir fry until onions turn light golden. Add *haldi* and dry red chilles. Stir. Add fresh coriander or curry leaves. Stir.
5. Add potatoes and salt. Mix well. Keeping the heat very low, cover tightly with a lid, and cook for 10-12 minutes or until the potatoes are tender.
6. Uncover and add chat masala. Adjust the seasonings. Transfer to a serving platter and serve hot.

Mexican Brinjals

Picture on back cover

Servings 8-10

- An attractive and delicious preparation of brinjals.

INGREDIENTS

2 longish brinjals of round variety
½ cup curd of full cream milk - hung for 15 minutes
chaat masala
coriander leaves or boiled peas to garnish
oil for frying

for the Mexican sauce

3 large tomatoes- chopped
1 large onion - finely chopped
6-7 flakes garlic - finely chopped
1 green chilli - finely chopped
2 tbsp tomato ketchup
dash of Tabasco sauce
1 tbsp oil
salt to taste
¼ tsp pepper
½ tsp red chilli powder

METHOD

1. Cut ¼" to ½" thick rounds of brinjals.
2. Soak in salted water for 15 minutes.
3. Wipe dry with a clean napkin.
4. Heat 3-4 tbsp oil in a non stick pan. Shallow fry the brinjals to a brown colour. Check that they get cooked properly.
5. Hang curd for 15 minutes in a thin muslin cloth.
6. Beat this curd with salt and pepper to taste.

for the Mexican sauce

1. Heat oil. Add onion and garlic and cook till onions turn pink.
2. Add tomatoes and other ingredients. Cook for 7-8 minutes till thick and dry. Mash a little.

to serve

1. Sprinkle *chaat masala* on the fried brinjals.
2. Arrange in a heat proof, flat serving plate.
3. Spread the prepared Mexican sauce on each piece of brinjal.
4. Dot with 1 tsp of the prepared curd.
5. Heat in a hot oven for about 7-8 minutes.
6. Top with coriander leaf or a pea and serve immediately.

Exciting Raita's

India being a hot country, curd is a desirable item in our meals. In this section, I have given you a few ideas which can change simple curds to tasty raitas. I am including some tips to set curd because a sour curd will not make a good raita.

- The milk should be luke warm.
- Very little starter (khatta), about half a tea spoon for half a kilo of milk is required.
- After the khatta has been added, mix well by pouring the milk from one vessel to another, two-three times.
- It takes three-four hours for the curd to set.
- As soon as the curd sets, keep the curd in the fridge.
- In winters, heat the milk a little more and add extra khatta.
- During winters, set the curd in a casserole to keep it warm.

Mixed Vegetable Raita

Servings 4-5

INGREDIENTS

½ kg (2½ cups) curd
1 onion - chopped finely
1 tomato - chopped finely
2 green chillies - chopped finely
½ carrot - grated
½ *kheera* (cucumber) grated
a pinch of powdered sugar
salt, black pepper to taste
1 tbsp of chopped coriander

METHOD

1. Beat curd.
2. Cut the tomato into four pieces, remove pulp and then chop finely.
3. Add all ingredients to the curd.
4. Serve cold.

Mint Raita

Servings 4-5

INGREDIENTS

½ kg curd (2½ cups curd)
½ cup of finely chopped *poodina* (mint) leaves
1 tsp powdered sugar
1 tbsp *kishmish* (raisins)
½ onion - chopped finely
1 tomato - chopped finely
1 green chilli - chopped finely
salt and red chilli powder to taste

METHOD

1. Beat curd well, preferably with an electric beater.
2. Wash *poodina* leaves well and chop finely.
3. Add all the ingredients to the curd. Mix well.
4. Keep in the fridge till serving time.

Raita Anaarkali

Servings 4-5

INGREDIENTS

½ kg curd - 2½ cups
1 cup *anaar ke dane* (fresh pomegranate seeds) - 1 big anaar
1 tsp roasted *zeera* (cumin seeds) powder
½ tsp chilli powder
salt to taste-½ tsp approx.

METHOD

1. Beat curd.
2. Mix all ingredients.
3. Keep in the fridge till serving time.

Attractive Papadi Raita

Picture on facing page Servings 4-5

- Prepare this raita in a round shallow dish with low sides.

INGREDIENTS

½ kg curd - 2½ cups
½ cup *boondi (besan ki)*
1 big boiled potato - cut into small pieces
½ tsp red chilli powder
1 tsp *zeera* (cumin seeds) powder
salt to taste

Other ingredients

1 packet of *papadi*
½ cup *imli* (tamarind) *ki chutney*
silver leaf, optional
fresh coriander

METHOD

1. Beat curd.
2. Add *boondi*, boiled potato, salt, *zeera* & red chilli powder.
3. Keep in a shallow round dish in the fridge.
4. At the time of serving, arrange 2-3 rows of *papadis* - standing upright on the sides.
5. Pour *imli ki chutney* on the *papadis*.
6. Gently stick some silver leaf on the *papadis*. Do not let the *papadis* slip into the *dahi*.
7. Put a bunch of uncut coriander leaves in the centre of the curd and make a ring of red chilli powder, surrounding it.
8. Serve immediately.

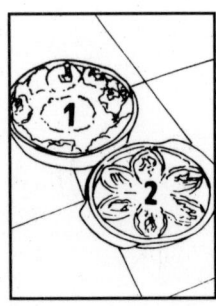

1. Attractive Papadi Raita — - Recipe on page 94
2. Kofta Rangeen — - Recipe on page 68

D̲ahi-B̲halle B̲emisaal

Servings 12 pieces

- The thorough beating of the ground dal makes all the difference.

INGREDIENTS

for the bhallas

1 cup *urad dhuli dal* (split black beans)
½" piece ginger
1 green chilli
2 pinches of *hing* asafoetida)

METHOD

for the bhallas

1. Clean, wash *dal*. Soak in water for about 4 hours.
2. Strain. Grind with minimum amount of water along with the other ingredients.
3. Beat the batter preferably with an electric beater or with your fingers, adding a tbsp of hot water 2 to 3 times, till whitish and frothy. Do not add too much water.
4. After beating, the mixture should look whitish frothy and a ball of this mixture should float when dropped in water.
5. Heat oil to medium hot temperature.
6. Wet your palms with a little water. Put a ball of the *dal* mixture on your left palm, push in one *kishmish* and flatten the ball. Transfer it gently on your wet, right hand fingers and slowly slip into the hot oil with the help of the thumb.
7. Deep fry 5-6 pieces at a time.
8. Heat 6 cups of water with 2 tsp salt. Drop 4-5 fried bhallas. Leave in water for ½ minute. Turn them. Remove from water after a few seconds.
9. Squeeze them gently. Keep in the fridge.

Contd...

Exciting Raita's

INGREDIENTS	METHOD

to prepare the dahi

½ kg (2½ cups) curd
salt to taste
½ tsp powdered sugar
1 tsp roasted *zeera* (cumin seeds) powder
½ tsp red chilli powder
¼ tsp kala namak

to prepare the dahi

1. Beat curd very well, preferably with an electric egg beater.
2. Add all the other ingredients.

to serve

1. Chill the prepared *dahi*.
2. Dip the prepared bhalle in *dahi* and arrange in a dish.
3. Pour extra *dahi* on top, at the time of serving.
4. Serve with tamarind (imli) chutney.

Note :
- Soak *dal* for a bout 4 hours.
- After grinding the *dal* in a grinder, beat the *dal* well, adding a few drops of hot water occasionally. The MORE YOU BEAT the *dal*, the better it is.
- Do not add salt to the *dal* mixture. Salt is added only in the water.
- No soda-bicarb should be added. The *bhallas* absorb a lot of oil if it is added.
- Fry the *bhalle* immediately after beating.

Baghara Raita

Servings 4-5

INGREDIENTS

½ kg (2½ cups) curd
½ cup grated coconut
1 cup shredded cabbage
¼" piece ginger - grated finely
2 green chillies - chopped finely
salt to taste

for the baghar

1 tbsp oil
½ tsp *sarson* (mustard seeds)
½ tsp *zeera* (cumin seeds)

METHOD

1. Beat curd.
2. Mix cabbage, coconut, ginger, green chillies and salt.
3. Heat 1 tbsp oil and add *zeera* & mustard seeds.
4. When they crackle, pour over the prepared *raita*.
5. Keep raita in the fridge.

Peanut Raita

Servings 4

INGREDIENTS

½ kg (2½ cups) curd
½ cup roasted, salted peanuts
1 small *kheera* - chopped
3-4 curry leaves
1 tbsp oil
¼ tsp red chilli powder

METHOD

1. Pound peanuts to a coarse powder.
2. Beat curd. Add *kheera*, peanuts & salt to taste.
3. Heat oil. Add curry leaves. Cook for a few seconds. Add chilli powder and remove from fire.
4. Pour over the prepared *raita*.
5. Mix and serve.

Chaawal - Roti

At the time of planning the menu, we should not side track the rotis, because the best of dishes may not taste their best if served with simple phulkas. An ordinary meal may turn into a special one, if served with tandoori paranthas, poodina paranthas or missi rotis. Always remember that the dough should be prepared at least half an hour before making the rotis. Similarly, rice should be soaked for at least half an hour before cooking it. A small clean towel napkin put under the lid of the pan prevents the rice from being sticky besides keeping it hot during the waiting period. The towel napkin absorbs moisture, and does not let the steam escape. Another thing which must be kept in mind is that rice should always be cooked in a heavy bottomed pan, with a tight fitting lid. Thus, a little thought over the cereals will enhance the taste of the food immensely.

Paneer & Mushroom Pulao

Picture on back cover

Servings 4

- Tastes delicious!

INGREDIENTS

1 cup *basmati* rice
100 gms mushrooms (½ packet)
150 gms *paneer* (cottage cheese)
1 onion - sliced finely
1 carrot - optional
1 capsicum - optional
2-3 *laung* (cloves)
1" stick *dalchini* (cinnamon)
1½ tsp salt
2 tbsp *desi ghee* or 3 tbsp oil

METHOD

1. Clean, wash rice. Soak for 1 hour.
2. Wash mushrooms thoroughly and cut each into thick slices lengthwise, into 'T' shaped pieces.
3. Cut *paneer* into ½" square pieces and deep fry to a golden colour.
4. Shred the carrot and capsicum into thin strips.
5. Heat *ghee*. Add *dalchini*, *laung* and onions. Cook till onions turn light brown in colour.
6. Add mushrooms. Cook for 3-4 minutes on low heat.
7. Add 2 cups of water. Add the strained rice, capsicum and carrot. Add *paneer*.
8. Add salt. Boil.
9. Cook covered on slow fire till the rice is done.

Mixed Vegetable Pulao

Serves 4

INGREDIENTS

1 cup uncooked rice - soaked for 1 hour
3 tbsp oil
1 tsp *jeera* (cumin seeds)
2-3 *laung* (clove)
2 moti *illaichi* (black cardamom)
1 small stick *dalchini* (cinnamon)
1 *tej patta* (bay leaf)
2 onions - thinly sliced
1½ tsp salt or to taste
½ cup shelled peas
1 small carrot - cut into small pieces
6-8 french beans - cut into small pieces

METHOD

1. Heat oil in a heavy bottomed pan. Reduce flame. Add *jeera, dalchini, tej patta, laung* and *moti illaichi*. Stir fry till *jeera* turns golden.
2. Add onions. Stir fry till they turn transparent.
3. Add the vegetables and salt. Stir fry for 3-4 minutes.
4. Add rice. Mix gently. Add 2 cups of water. Boil.
5. Cover and cook on very low heat for 12-15 minutes, until the water is absorbed and the rice is done.

L<small>EMON</small> R<small>ICE</small>

Picture on page 25 *Servings 2-3*

- The South Indian speciality.

INGREDIENTS

1 cup basmati rice
3-4 tbsp oil
juice of one large lemon
1 tsp *rai* (mustard seeds)
1 tbsp *chnane ki dal* (split gram)
1½ tsp salt
½ tsp *haldi* (turmeric powder)
2-3 green chillies - slit
10-12 *curry pattas*

METHOD

1. Clean, wash and **soak rice for 1 hour**.
2. Heat oil in a heavy bottomed pan.
3. Add mustard seeds & *channe ki dal*. Remove from fire. Add *curry pattas*.
4. Return to very slow fire & cook till *dal* turns golden brown.
5. Measure 2 cups water carefully and add to the *dal*. Add salt & *haldi*.
6. Add lemon juice. Boil water.
7. Strain the rice and add to the water as soon as it boils. Add green chillies.
8. Keep a *tawa* under the pan of rice.
9. Cover with a small towel napkin and then a lid.
10. Cook on low heat till the rice is done.
11. Serve hot with *sambhar* or curd.

Missi - Roti

Servings 5-6 roti

- Besani roti flavoured with kasoori methi.

INGREDIENTS	METHOD
1 cup *besan* (gram flour) 1 cup *atta* (whole wheat flour) 2 tbsp oil or melted *ghee* 1 tbsp *kasoori methi* (dry fenugreek leaves) ½ tsp salt ½ tsp red chilli powder ½ tsp *zeera* (cumin seeds) a pinch of *hing* (asafoetida) a pinch of *haldi* (tumeric powder)	1. Mix all ingredients. Add enough water to make a dough of rolling consistency. 2. Cover it and keep aside for ½ hour. 3. Make 6 balls. 4. Roll each ball into a *chappati*, but thicker than the usual *chappati*. 5. Cook on a hot *tawa* by frying it or in a hot *tandoor*. 6. When made in a *tandoor*, apply *ghee* and serve immediately.

Vegetable Biryani

Picture on page 67   *Servings 5-6*

- Different ingredients blend together to make it wonderful.

INGREDIENTS

2 cups *basmati* rice
1-2 carrots - cut daigonally into slices
1 small cauliflower - cut into medium florets
8-10 french beans-1" long diagonally cut pieces
2 small potatoes - cut into fours
2 onions - sliced finely
½ cup oil
3 tsp salt
1 tsp lemon juice
1 *tej patta* (bay leaf)

to grind to a paste

6-7 flakes garlic
1" piece ginger
1 tbsp *saunf* (aniseeds)
1 tsp *zeera* (cumin seeds)
3 red chillies
1 tsp *dhania* (coriander) powder
1" stick of *dalchini* (cinnamon)
3-4 *laung* (cloves)
3-4 *saboot kali mirch* (peppercorns)
seeds of 2 *moti illaichi* (brown cardamoms)

METHOD

1. Soak rice for **1 hour**.
2. Grind the ingredients of the paste together with a little water.
3. Heat oil in a heavy bottomed pan. Add onions, cook till golden brown.
4. Add the paste and *tej patta*.
5. Add the vegetables and stir fry for 3-4 minutes.
6. Measure 4 cups of water and add to the vegetables.
7. Add salt and lemon juice.
8. When water boils, strain the rice and add to the water.
9. Put a *tawa* under the pan of rice.
10. Cover the pan of rice with a small towel napkin and then with a well fitting lid. Keep some heavy weight, on the lid.
11. Slow down the fire and cook till the rice is done (10-15 minutes).

Methi Wali Puri or Parantha

Servings 10-15

Picture on page 61

- Delicious parathas!

INGREDIENTS

2½ cups *atta* (whole wheat flour)
1½ cups - 250 gms *methi* (fenugreek leaves) - chopped finely
2 tbsp oil
1 tsp salt
½ tsp red chilli powder
½ tsp *garam masala* (mixed spices)
½ tsp *ajwain* (carom seeds)

METHOD

1. Chop *methi* leaves finely. Mix ½ tsp salt and keep aside for 1 hour.
2. Squeeze *methi*. Wash several times. Squeeze again to remove water.
3. Mix *methi* with other ingredients.
4. Knead to a dough of rolling consistency with enough water. Keep aside for ½ hour.
5. For *paranthas*, make balls, roll slightly, spread *ghee* nicely all over. Fold into half, then again into half to get a triangle.
6. Roll out. Cook on a *tawa*, fry with a little *ghee*.
7. If *puris* are to be made, keep the dough a little stiffer than the *paratha* dough and deep fry in oil.

Vegetable Fried Rice

Servings 2

INGREDIENTS

1 cup *basmati* rice
2 tsp salt
50 gms white mushrooms
50 gms *paneer* (cottage cheese)
1 small carrot
½ cup boiled peas green stalks of 2-3 spring onions
1 tsp ginger juice
½ tsp white pepper
½ tsp red chilli powder
5 tbsp oil

METHOD

1. Wash, soak rice for ½ hour.
2. Boil 5-6 cups of water with 2 tsp salt.
3. Strain the soaked rice and add to the boiling water.
4. Boil till done. Keep in a strainer for 5-7 minutes.
5. Add 2 tsp oil to the rice. Mix gently. Keep away for at least ½ hour. In-between fluff the rice with a fork to keep the grains of the rice separate.
6. Cut *paneer* into ½" cubes.
7. Cut carrots into tiny cubes.
8. Boil peas in salted water.
9. Cut mushrooms into two or leave them whole if small.
10. Cut spring onion stalks into diagonal, thin, long pieces.
11. Heat 5 tbsp oil. Fry *paneer* and keep aside.
12. Fry mushrooms for 3-4 minutes on high flame. Remove from oil.
13. Fry carrots, peas, onion stalks separately in batches and remove from oil.
14. In a clean *karahi* add 2 tbsp oil. Fry the rice for 2-3 minutes.
15. Add fried vegetables, ½ tsp salt, ½ black pepper, red chilli powder and ginger juice to the rice.
16. Mix well and stir for 2-3 minutes.

Note : To take out ginger juice, grate 1" ginger piece and squeeze through a muslin cloth.

Desserts - Puddings

A delicious dessert can turn a meal into a treat. Here is a treasury of recipes which includes, classic elegant sweets like souffles and trifles, as well as the all time favourites like malpua-kheer, pista-illaichi kulfi and so on... A light dessert should follow a heavy dinner, where as a rich dessert is enjoyed by all after a light meal. Rich or light, the dessert should be so beautifully decorated that when it comes on the table to be served, you are unable to take your eyes off it. If you are good at cream icing, beautifying the desserts is no problem. A few swirls of cream here and there, do magic. In case you cannot manage the icing, do not get disheartened. You can always decorate the dessert with fresh fruits, sauces and tinned cherries. Other simple ways of decoration are given along with the desserts.

Apple Stew with Rabri

Picture on page 109 *Servings 6*

- A great combination of the East and the West!

INGREDIENTS

to stew apples

3 apples
3 cups water
4 tbsp sugar
1 tsp lemon juice
½ stick *dalchini* (cinnamon)

for the custard

3 cups apple syrup
3 tbsp sugar
3 tbsp custard powder

METHOD

to stew apples

1. Peel apples. Cut into equal halves. Remove seeds.
2. Boil water with sugar, lemon juice & *dalchini*.
3. Add the apple pieces. Cook, covered for 3-4 minutes till apples turn soft.
4. Remove the apples from the syrup and transfer the apples to a dish. Reserve the syrup. Strain the syrup and keep aside.

to prepare custard

1. Dissolve custard powder in ½ cup syrup.
2. Boil the left over syrup with sugar.
3. Add the dissolved custard, stirring continuously.
4. Boil till translucent and slightly thick (5-6 minutes).
5. Pour over the apples placed in a serving dish. Chill. Sprinkle shredded *pista* in the centre of each apple.
6. Serve chilled with rabri as given on the next page.

Contd...

1. Apple Stew	- Recipe on page 108
2. Rabri	- Recipe on page 110
3. Orange Turn about	- Recipe on page 119

Rabri

Picture on page 109

- Relish it by itself or with stewed apples as given on page 108

INGREDIENTS

½ kg - (2½ cups) of full cream milk
4 tbsp milk powder
2½ tbsp sugar
2 tbsp fresh *malai*
a few *pistas* (pistachio)
silver leaf, optional

METHOD

1. Boil milk in a *karahi*.
2. Mix milk powder in a little hot milk so that it is lumpy and not smooth.
3. Add the milk powder paste, sugar & *malai* to the milk in the *karahi*.
4. Cook for 30 minutes on low heat till it turns thick. Cool. Serve chilled in a separate dish, decorated with shredded *pista* and silver leaf.

Chocolate Exotica

Servings 8

- A treat! Chocolate cake sandwiched with cherries in cream, topped with ice cream and chocolate sauce.

INGREDIENTS

for the sponge cake

4 large eggs
3/4 cup (75 gms) *maida* (plain flour)
1 tea cup (115 gm) sifted powdered sugar
1 tsp baking powder
¼ cup cocoa
1 tsp vanilla essence
1½ tbsp hot boiling water

for the cherry cream filling

150 gms (3/4 cup) cream
4 tbsp powdered sugar
3/4 cup tinned cherries
½ tsp vanilla essence

METHOD

for the sponge cake

1. Beat whites of egg in a dry pan, till stiff.
2. Add sifted sugar gradually, beating after each addition.
3. Mix in the egg yolks. Beat.
4. Add hot water in drops. Keep beating at the same time.
5. Sift *maida*, baking powder and cocoa.
6. Add the sifted *maida* gradually, 2-3 tbsp at a time to the egg mixture. Gently fold the *maida*.
7. Add essence. Fold. Do not beat.
8. Bake in a preheated oven at 200°C for ½ hour in a greased tin of 8-9" diameter.

for the cherry cream filling

1. Beat cream with sugar till thick.
2. Stone, chop cherries and add to cream.
3. Mix in the essence.

Contd...

Date and Walnut Pudding

Servings 6

INGREDIENTS

½ tin milk-maid (condensed milk)
½ cup (80 gms) butter
250 gms dates
85 gms (a little more than 3/4 cup) *maida*
½ cup chopped walnuts
½ tsp vanilla essence
½ tsp soda-bicarb
1 tsp baking powder

Custard Sauce

2½ cups (½ kg) milk
3 tbsp sugar
1 heaped tbsp custard powder

METHOD

1. Remove seeds from dates and chop them finely.
2. Soak chopped dates in 5 tbsp of water with ½ tsp soda-bicarb for 4-5 hours or overnight.
3. Sift *maida* with baking powder. Add dates and walnuts to the *maida*. Mix well.
4. Beat milk-maid and butter well, in a clean pan.
5. Add the maida mixture to the milk-maid mixture. Add essence and beat well.
6. Bake in a preheated oven at 150°C for 45-50 minutes. Keep aside.
7. Prepare custard sauce by dissolving custard powder in ½ cup milk.
8. Heat the remaining 2 cups of milk with sugar. When it boils, add the custard powder, stirring continuously.
9. Cook for a few minutes till it coats the back of the spoon.
10. Serve the pudding with hot custard sauce.

Ice Cream with Apples in Hot Cherry Sauce

Servings 6

- A light, refreshing dessert!

INGREDIENTS

for stewing the apples

6 medium sized apples
1½ cups water
12 tsp sugar
1 tsp lemon juice

for the cherry sauce

½ cup syrup of the apples
1½ tsp cornflour
4-5 glace cherries - cut into thin slices
a drop of dark pink (strawberry red) colour
1 tsp lemon juice

to serve

6 stewed apple pieces
½ cup cherry sauce
1 litre vanilla ice cream

METHOD

for stewing the apples

1. Place the sugar, water and lemon juice in a wide sauce pan.
2. Peel the apples, then cut in half. Scoop out the seeds (core the apple).
3. Boil the sugar and water. Place the apples, flat side down in the syrup.
4. Boil the apples for about 10 minutes till the apples become soft. Chill the apples.

for the cherry sauce

1. Remove the apples from the syrup.
2. To ½ cup of syrup add cornflour & mix well.
3. Simmer syrup on fire till the sauce attains a coating consistency.
4. Remove from fire, add enough colour to get a pale pink colour.
5. Add glaced cherries and lemon juice.

to serve

1. Place a slab of vanilla ice cream in an individual plate or bowl.
2. Arrange an apple piece on it.
3. Pour warm cherry sauce over it. Serve immediately.

Strawberry Ripple Pudding

Servings 6

INGREDIENTS

for the custard

3 cups milk
3 tbsp custard powder
3 tbsp sugar
1 tsp vanilla essence

other ingredients

2 cups - (400 gms) fresh cream
8 tbsp powdered sugar
1 packet strawberry jelly
1 small tin of cherries
12 Marie biscuits

METHOD

1. Prepare jelly according to the instructions given on the packet.
2. Cool the jelly. Set in the freezer.
3. Dissolve custard powder in ½ cup milk.
4. Boil 2½ cups of milk with sugar. Add the dissolved custard, stirring continuously.
5. Cook till it coats the back of the spoon. Cool. Add essence. Chill.
6. Beat cream with powdered sugar till thick. Fold into the custard.
7. In a transparent bowl, spread half of custard.
8. Beat jelly and spread on the custard.
9. Soak biscuits in cherry syrup and place over the jelly.
10. Remove seeds of cherries and arrange on the biscuits.
11. Cover with jelly.
12. Top with remaining custard.
13. Spread some cherries on the top.

Mango Pie

Picture on facing page

Servings 8-10

- Enjoy the mango flavour even without fresh mangoes.

INGREDIENTS

base

a flan dish (loose bottomed tin)
20 "Good-day" biscuits - ground to a powder
8 tbsp of melted white butter

other ingredients

2 packets - (400 ml) mango fruity drink
7 tbsp sugar
4 tsp gelatine
½ cup water
300 gm (1½ cups) cream

topping

fresh mangoes, if available
some cherries or grapes to decorate

METHOD

1. Put the ground biscuits in a bowl. Add the melted butter and mix well. Add enough butter such that the mixture binds easily. Spread at the bottom of a loose bottomed tin. Press well and keep the tin on a plate and refrigerate for atleast 1 hour to set well.
2. Sprinkle 4 tsp gelatine on ½ cup water kept in a small heavy bottomed pan. Heat on slow fire to dissolve it. Keep aside.
3. In a separate pan mix mango fruity and sugar. Keep on fire for a few minutes to dissolve sugar. Remove from fire.
4. Add the gelatine solution to the lukewarm fruity. Cool.
5. Chill in the freezer, till thick but not set.
6. Beat the thickened fruity. Add cream.
7. Beat once again and pour over the set biscuit crust. Freeze till firm for about 2-3 hours.
8. Remove dessert from tin and place on the serving dish along with the tin base.
9. Garnish with mangoes and cherries, if available. Make a border of biscuit crumbs. Keep in the fridge till serving time.
10. 15 minutes before serving, return to the freezer to chill it properly.
11. To serve, cut into wedges.

for the chocolate sauce

½ cup water
1 tbsp cocoa
1½ tbsp sugar
1½ tsp cornflour
1 tsp butter (white)

to prepare chocolate exotica

½ litre vanilla ice cream
½ kg chocolate sponge cake
½ cup chocolate sauce
½ cup cherry syrup
1 tsp brandy essence or rum

for the chocolate sauce

1. Mix all ingredients together.
2. Cook on low heat till the sauce attains a coating consistency. Remove from fire.
3. Cool.

to prepare chocolate exotica

1. Divide the cake into two pieces.
2. Add brandy essence or rum to cherry syrup.
3. Soak both the pieces of cake with the syrup.
4. Put softened ice cream in the empty cake tin. Level it.
5. Place a piece of cake over it.
6. Spread cherry cream over it.
7. Place the second piece of cake. Press. Cover the tin with aluminium foil.
8. Freeze for 6-7 hours at least.
9. An hour before serving, unmould the ice cream on to a serving plate, pour cold chocolate sauce over it in swirls and freeze again.
10. Decorate with tinned cherries and whipped cream.

Note : • This dessert can be prepared 3-4 days in advance for a party. Cover the dessert well with aluminium foil and keep in the freezer.

Baked Guavas with Cream

Servings 6

- The flavour of baked guavas is irresistible!

INGREDIENTS

6 medium, fresh, ripe guavas of good quality
6 tsp sugar
250 gm cream
3-4 drops vanilla essence
6 tbsp powdered sugar
1 tbsp chopped *kaju* (cashew nuts)
1 tbsp finely chopped almonds
3 glaced cherries

METHOD

1. Peel guavas. Slice off an ½" thick piece from the top. Scoop out the seeds with a spoon.
2. Sprinkle 1 tsp of sugar in each guava and spread it nicely on the inner surface with a spoon.
3. Bake in a preheated oven at 200°C for about 15-20 minutes till they become soft. Do not let them become limp by being in the oven for a longer time. Cool. Keep in the fridge.
4. Beat cream with sugar and essence till soft peaks are formed. Fill some cream in an icing bag for decoration, if desired.
5. Mix nuts in the beaten cream. Chill.
6. Fill guavas with cream. Top with a swirl of beaten cream in the icing gun. Decorate with half a cherry.
7. Serve on a bed of thin cream in a low sided dish.

Desserts - Puddings

Orange Turn About

Picture on page 109

Servings 6

INGREDIENTS

- 1 packet orange jelly
- 1½ cups water
- 2 tbsp sugar
- 1½ cups (250 gm) cream
- 4-5 drops orange colour
- ½ cup tinned cherries
- 3-4 fresh oranges
- 2 tbsp powdered sugar
- 1 tbsp orange marmalade
- 1 tsp cornflour

Note:
You may use strawberry jelly instead of orange jelly to make "Strawberry Turn About" of a bright pink colour as shown on the cover.

METHOD

1. Mix jelly, water and 2 tbsp sugar in a pan.
2. Heat on slow fire, stirring continuously, till jelly dissolves.
3. Remove from fire. Cool.
4. After it cools completely, add 1 cup cream, keeping aside ½ cup. Add orange colour.
5. Rinse a ring mould. Pour ¾ of the jelly in it. Set in the freezer. Keep the left over jelly in the fridge.
6. Remove seeds of cherries and skin of orange segments. Mix some powdered sugar to the oranges if they are sour.
7. When the jelly sets, place a few (¼ of the total amt.) of cherries and oranges on the set jelly.
8. Beat the left over jelly and pour over the fruits. Keep in the fridge till set.
9. Unmould by running a knife on the inner and outer ring of the mould. Dip for a second in warm water kept in a plate.
10. Unmould on to a flat serving plate.
11. Fill the centre with oranges or any fruit of your chioce. Dust with powdered sugar.
12. Beat ½ cup cream with 2 tbsp of powdered sugar to form soft peaks. Fill the whipped cream in an icing bag and keep in the freezer for 8-10 minutes.
13. Pipe stars on the jelly with whipped cream.
14. Melt orange marmalade or any jam with 2 tbsp of water and cornflour on low flame till it attains a saucy consistency. Pour over the fruits. Serve chilled.

Pineapple Trifle

Servings 8

INGREDIENTS

for the custard

2½ tbsp custard powder
425 ml (2¼ cups) milk
1/3 cup (50 gms) sugar

Other ingredients

1 small tin pineapple slices
1 packet pineapple flavoured jelly
½ kg sponge cake - pineapple flavoured
1 tbsp almonds - chopped

METHOD

1. Dissolve custard powder in ¼ cup milk. Boil 2 cups milk with sugar.
2. Add custard stirring continuously. Cook for 5-6 minutes. Chill.
3. Drain and chop pineapple into small bits.
4. Heat 2½ cups of pineapple syrup. Add it to the jelly crystals. Mix well to dissolve the crystals.
5. Cool the jelly.
6. Cut cake into thin ½" pieces and line a sided dish (bottom & sides).
7. Spread pineapple pieces.
8. Pour the cooled jelly. Keep in the freezer till set.
9. Beat the chilled custard and pour over the set jelly. Chill.
10. Sprinkle chopped almonds.
11. Serve chilled.

Shahi Kulfi

Servings 15

- The simple way of making kulfis.

INGREDIENTS

1 kg (5 cups) full cream milk - at room temp.
1 tin (400 gms) milkmaid (condensed milk)
2 tbsp cornflour
3-4 *chhoti illaichi* (green cardamoms) - crushed
1 tbsp shredded *pista* (pistachio)
1 tbsp shredded almonds

METHOD

1. Open the tin of milkmaid in a heavy bottomed pan.
2. Dissolve cornflour in ¼ cup milk.
3. Add the rest of the milk gradually to the milk-maid, stirring continuously.
4. Mix well. Add *illaichi*. Keep on fire. Boil.
5. Add the cornflour paste to the boiling milk, stirring continuously.
6. Continue boiling, by lowering the flame, for about 5 minutes. Remove from fire. Cool.
7. Add *pista* and almonds.
8. Fill in clean kulfi moulds and leave to set in the freezer for 6-8 hours or overnight.

Shahi Kulfi-II

Servings 8

- Yet another simple way to make kulfis.

INGREDIENTS

1 kg (5 cups) full cream milk
¼ cup + 1 tbsp sugar
3 tbsp cornflour
5 tbsp milk powder
1 tbsp *pista* (pistachio) - very finely cut
1 tbsp (8-10) almonds - very finely cut
3-4 crushed *chhoti illaichi* (green cardamom)
4-5 threads *kesar*, optional

METHOD

1. Dissolve cornflour in ½ cup cold milk and keep aside.
2. Put rest of the milk on fire in a *karahi*. Add *illaichi, kesar* and sugar.
3. Dissolve milk powder in a little luke warm milk taken from the *karahi* on fire.
4. Boil the milk in the *karahi*.
5. Add cornflour-milk powder paste to boiling milk.
6. Boil for 20 minutes on medium flame till it is reduced to 2½-3 cups.
7. Keep stirring in-between and scraping the thickened milk from the sides of the *karahi*. This gives the *rabri* in the kulfi.
8. Remove from fire. Cool.
9. Add almonds, *pista* and crushed *illaichi*.
10. Fill the mixture in the *kulfi* moulds. Freeze for 6-8 hours or overnight.

Chocolate Pudding

Servings 4

- Extremely simple!

INGREDIENTS

2 cups milk
2 tsp gelatine
8 tsp sugar
1 tsp honey
1½ tbsp custard powder
3 tbsp cocoa
1 cup (200 gms) cream
1 small milk chocolate
walnut halves for decoration

METHOD

1. Mix custard powder and cocoa in ¼ cup milk.
2. Put the rest of the milk with sugar on fire.
3. When it boils, add the dissolved custard, stirring continuously. Cook for 2-3 minutes only, to make a very thin custard. Do not over cook.
4. Mix gelatine in ¼ cup water. Heat on low flame to dissolve it.
5. Add the gelatine to the chocolate custard stirring continuously. Add honey.
6. Cool the custard by keeping the pan over cold water.
7. Mix ½ cup cream (keeping aside ½ cup for the decoration) with the cooled chocolate custard.
8. Keep in the freezer, touching the bottom of the freezer, till set (½ hour).
9. Decorate with whipped cream, chocolate flakes and walnut halves.
10. Remove from freezer & keep on the first shelf of the refrigerator.
11. The pudding should be chilled again in the freezer for 15 minutes just before serving.

Note :
- The gelatine should not be more than 6 months old. See the manufacturing date before purchasing it.
- To decorate the pudding beautifully with cream and chocolate flakes, refer to my book – "Vegetarian Wonders".

Cake n' Ice Cream Fantasia

Servings 8

- Simply fantastic!

INGREDIENTS

½ kg pineapple sponge cake
½ litre vanilla ice cream
2 tbsp orange jam or marmalade
150 gms cream - chilled
3 tbsp powdered sugar
1 big apple - peeled, cut into small flat pieces
½ cup water
2 tbsp sugar
½ tsp lemon juice
½ cup chocolate sauce

METHOD

1. Split cake into two equal halves.
2. Spread 1 tbsp of jam or marmalade on each piece.
3. Boil ½ cup water with 2 tbsp sugar & lemon juice. Add apple pieces.
4. Cook for 2 minutes till apples are soft. Cool.
5. Beat cream with 3 tbsp powdered sugar till thick. Add apples, reserving the syrup.
6. In the empty cake tin put the softened ice cream.
7. Place a piece of cake on it with the jam side touching the ice cream.
8. Soak the cake with apple syrup. Spread apples in cream over it.
9. Press the other piece of cake on it with the jam side down. Soak with syrup.
10. Cover with aluminium foil & freeze for 6-8 hours. This can be kept for a few days.
11. Unmould 1 hour before serving.
12. Make swirls of chocolate sauce on the ice cream which now comes on top after inverting the dessert. Freeze again.
13. Serve within a few hours.

Crumbly Grape Pudding

Servings 4-5

- The simplest dessert which you can prepare when you are short of time.

INGREDIENTS

10-12 choccolate chip biscuits
100 gms black grapes
100 gms green grapes
300 gms (1½ cups) fresh cream - chilled
4 tbsp powdered sugar
2 tsp brown sugar - optional

METHOD

1. Whip chilled cream till thick & soft peaks form.
2. Crush biscuits coarsely with the fingers.
3. Wash, slit grapes into halves.
4. In a transparent bowl, put 1/3 of the cream.
5. Then put a few tbsps of the biscuit crumbs.
6. Spread some grapes over it.
7. Spread ½ of cream again.
8. Cover it with a thin layer of biscuit crumbs.
9. Spread some grapes.
10. Spread the left over cream.
11. Top with a few grapes sprinkled with brown sugar. Chill.

Nita Mehta's BEST SELLING COOKERY BOOKS

1. All-time Favourite SNACKS
2. Best of CHINESE Vegetarian Cuisine
3. BREAKFAST Special
4. Breakfast & Brunch (Non Veg.)
5. Cakes & Chocolates
6. Continental Vegetarian Cooking
7. Chutneys, Squashes, Pickles
8. CHINESE Non Vegetarian
9. CHINESE cooking for the Indian kitchen
10. CONTINENTAL cooking for the Indian kitchen
11. Dal & Roti
12. Desserts & Puddings
13. Different Ways With CHAAWAL
14. Delicious Parlour ICE CREAMS
15. Delicious ZERO-OIL Cook Book
16. Delicious THAI Cookery
17. DINNER MENUS rom around the world
18. Favourite Non Vegetarian Dishes
19. Flavours of INDIAN COOKING (Hard Cover)
20. Green Vegetables
21. Indian Cooking - Handi Tawa Kadhai
22. Healthy & Delicious FOOD FOR CHILDREN
23. Indian Vegetarian Cookbook
24. JHATPAT KHAANA
25. Low Calorie Desserts
26. Low Calorie Recipes
27. LOW FAT Tasty Recipes
28. LOW CALORIE cooking for the Indian kitchen
29. MICROWAVE Non Vegetarian Cookery
30. MICROWAVE Vegetarian Cookery
31. MICROWAVE cooking for the Indian kitchen
32. MUGHLAI Vegetarian Cookery
33. MUGHLAI Non-Vegetarian Khaana
34. More Paneer
35. Non Veg. Low Calorie Recipes
36. Navratri Special Recipes
37. PANEER All the way
38. Party Food
39. Pasta & Corn
40. Perfect Vegetarian Cookery
41. PRESSURE COOKING
42. PUNJABI KHAANA (Hard Cover)
43. PUNJABI KHAANA (Paper Back)
44. Quick Meals
45. SNACKS Non Vegetarian
46. Soups Salads & Starters
47. South Indian Favourites
48. Sandwiches
49. Starters & Mocktails
50. The Art of BAKING
51. The Best of VEGETARIAN DISHES
52. The Best of CHICKEN Recipes
53. Taste of PUNJAB
54. Taste of GUJARAT
55. Taste of RAJASTHAN
56. Taste of KASHMIR
57. Tempting SNACKS
58. Vegetarian Wonders

Malpuas

Servings 4

- The Indian speciality for the rainy season! Serve with kheer given on the next page.

INGREDIENTS

8 tbsp *maida* (plain flour)
2 tbsp *suji* (semolina)
¼ tsp baking powder
3-4 tbsp *malai*
½ cup milk (approx)
seeds of 2 *chhoti illaichi* - crushed
2 tbsp *desi ghee*
½ tsp *til* (sesame seeds) - optional
5-6 *pistas* for decoration

Sugar Syrup

1/3 cup sugar
½ cup water
2 *chhoti illiachi* - crushed

METHOD

1. Mix *maida*, *suji*, baking powder and *malai* in a bowl.
2. Add milk gradually, mixing well, to get a batter of a soft dropping consistency, almost like a thick pouring consistency.
3. Add *chhoti illaichi* & beat well with a spoon for 2 minutes. Keep aside.
4. Prepare sugar syrup by boiling sugar, water and *illaichi* in a pan. After the syrups boils, keep on low heat for 5 minutes. Remove from heat & keep aside.
5. To prepare the *malpuas*, heat a nonstick *tawa*. Reduce flame. Spread 1 tsp *ghee* on it.
6. Drop 1 tbsp full of batter & spread it gently to a small disc of 2½"-3" diameter. Put more spoons of batter spacing them apart. Keep the flame low.
7. Sprinkle same *til* on the *puas*.
8. Pour ½ tsp melted *ghee* on each *pua*.
9. Cook on medium heat till edges turn brown. Turn the *puas* & cook till the other side also gets brown specs.
10. Put half of the *puas* in hot sugar syrup & keep it soaked for 2 minutes. Transfer to a serving platter. Soak the left over *puas* also. Keep the syrup aside in a bowl.
11. Garnish them with nuts.
12. At serving time, pour the left over syrup with a spoon on the puas. Warm in an oven or a microwave.

Special Rice-Kheer

Servings 4-5

- An excellent kheer with left over boiled rice.

INGREDIENTS

1 cup boiled rice
1 kg (5 cups) full cream milk
1/3 cup sugar
2 tbsp milk powder - dissolved in a little milk
3-4 *chhoti illaichi* (green cardamoms) - crushed
10-12 almonds - shredded
8-10 *pista* (pistachio) - shredded
1 tbsp *kishmish* (raisins)
1 silver leaf, optional

METHOD

1. Add cooked (boiled) rice to milk. Boil. Slow down the fire.
2. Add sugar, milk powder paste and *illaichi*. Cook on low flame till thick.
3. Keep mashing occasionally to break the rice grains.
4. When it reaches the right consistency, (thick pouring) add nuts and *kishmish*, keeping aside a few for the top.
5. Pour into a serving dish. Decorate with silver leaf. Spread whole almonds and shredded *pista*.
6. Serve hot *kheer* during the winter & rainy months and chilled *kheer* during the hot summer days.